Throttle Full Open

To Mary's second son, Jim Bailey CBE, DFC, MA,
and his wife Barbara, without whose encouragement, practical help
and enthusiasm this book would never have been written,
and to Valerie and Thomas Pakenham,
who introduced me to Jim and Barbara in the first place

Throttle Full Open

A Life of Lady Bailey, Irish Aviatrix

Jane Falloon

THE LILLIPUT PRESS

First published 1999 by
THE LILLIPUT PRESS LTD
62-63 Sitric Road, Arbour Hill,
Dublin 7, Ireland.

A CIP record for this
title is available from
The British Library.

ISBN 1 901866 43 2

Set in 11 on 14 Caslon
Map by Graham Thew Design
Printed in Ireland by Betaprint of Clonshaugh, Dublin

Tel No
01 6711647

Contents

Illustrations

Illustrations

1

Mary's Background

Mary Westenra was born on the first of December 1890, in 30 Grosvenor Square, London, the house of her maternal grandfather. She was the first child of Derrick – always known as Derry – the fifth Baron Rossmore of Ireland, the fourth Baron Rossmore of England, and his wife, Mittie. Derry was the owner of an imposing castle on an extensive estate in Co. Monaghan, Ireland. It was sometimes known as Rossmore Park and sometimes as Rossmore Castle; in the town of Monaghan it was simply 'the Castle'. Mittie came from the even more splendid Hooton Hall, in Cheshire, England. She was the daughter of Richard Christopher Naylor, a wealthy banker.

Both houses had been greatly enlarged and improved earlier in the nineteenth century. Rossmore Castle, built in 1827 in Tudor–Gothic style, had been made grander and more fantastical in 1858 by Derry's father, who had added towers, turrets, balustrades and battlements, turning it into a fairy-tale Scottish Renaissance castle. Hooton had been transformed by Mary's Naylor grandfather from a sober Georgian-fronted mansion into a structure of enormous size and splendour, with a vast sculpture gallery and an ornamented roofscape.

At the time of his daughter Mittie's marriage to Derry, Richard Naylor was a man of considerable wealth. His family was connected with a small bank in Liverpool, Leyland and Bullen. He had inherited a substantial fortune from his mother's brother, whose surname was Leyland. And he was involved in the cotton industry. In addition to Hooton Hall, he owned Kelmarsh Hall, in Northamptonshire, and Downshire House, in Belgrave Square, which is now the Spanish Embassy. At one time his London house was Hurlingham, in Fulham, now the Hurlingham Club. He was an enthusiastic sportsman and a successful owner of racehorses.

When Mary was born Derry was probably feeling at his most confident about his prospects and standing in the world. He was thirty-eight years old, married to the daughter of an extremely rich man who had bred only two daughters and no sons to inherit his wealth; he was the inheritor, through his older brother's death, of an estate of nearly fifteen thousand acres, and of a most impressive house filled with superb furniture; he employed a great number of servants; he was a peer of both realms; and he was possessed of a cheerful and gregarious temperament. His wife Mittie, as well as being an heiress, was very handsome and a good horsewoman; she came from a most socially acceptable background and moved in the top circles of English society.

Mary was not born until Derry and Mittie had been married for eight years. Perhaps there were earlier miscarriages to account for this long delay, which would have made Mary's arrival a source of particular relief and happiness to her parents. Ideally, of course, she should have been a boy, to guarantee an heir to her father's title. But this small disappointment must have been quickly over-shadowed by the happy realization that she was a healthy child and, as an added bonus, extremely pretty.

Although she was born in London, most of her childhood was spent in Ireland, at Rossmore Castle. On the first floor of the house there would have been a suite of rooms known as the nurs-ery wing, consisting of a day-nursery, a night nursery, a bedroom for the nurse or nanny, and probably a little scullery. There would have been a full-time nurse or nanny, with complete charge of every aspect of Mary's life, from her food and clothes to her health and manners and behaviour, as well as at least one, if not two, nursery maids to do the more mundane work of washing and iron-ing and bringing up the meals from the kitchens below. Mary would have been cocooned in this little world, seeing her mother when she was taken down to the drawing-room before her bedtime, dressed in her prettiest dress, expected to behave perfectly for that short time, for the amusement of her mother's guests – a small performer, to be laughed at, but not petted or loved. Any warmth would come from Nanny upstairs, and perhaps if Nanny were a dour Scot, who didn't approve of soft silly ways, there would be no hugs there either. Such a childhood might partly account for Mary's distant relationship with her own children, who never felt their mother showed them adequate affection.

Rossmore Castle must have been frightening for a small child in the dark winter evenings, as the long passages, filled with portraits and sculpture, gradually turned into dark caverns of menacing presences and flickering shadows. When Mary was very tiny her nurse accompanied her down to the drawing-room after tea, but as she grew older she must often have ventured out on her own, and found her way down to the vast kitchens and sculleries and game larders, which, every year in the shooting season, were hung with pheasant and hares and woodcock shot by her father and his friends.

The drawing-room was enormous. It had been built by Mary's great-grandfather, the second Lord Rossmore, when he finally came into his inheritance, in 1827. He had a neighbour, a Mr E.J. Shirley, who was building a huge house for himself called Lough Fea, a few miles from Rossmore. The two men – whether from animosity or fun – decided to compete with each other as to who could build the larger room. Lord Rossmore enlarged his drawing-room five times in order to be the victor, but was finally defeated when his building reached the edge of a cliff. Mr Shirley meanwhile had victoriously built on a great hall with a lofty hammerbeam roof, a minstrel's gallery, and an arcade at first-floor level – larger by several yards than the Rossmore drawing-room. Mary's niece Brigid Westenra remembers the huge room cluttered with fine furniture and with three beautiful glass chandeliers suspended from the ceiling. Peter Somerville-Large has described the room as it would have been in Mary's childhood: 'Photographs of the period show the great drawing-room cluttered with tables and chairs, crocheted antimacassars on fat sofas covered with chintz or linen, windows framed by heavy curtains and pelmets that looked as if they would pull down the house, ferns, palms, and perhaps a painting on an easel.'

Later, as Mary grew older, she would become familiar with the library – a lovely room, its walls lined with leather-bound books, overlooking the lawn. She ran up and down the enormous polished-wood main staircase. She must have been half terrified of all the gaunt figures, in coats of armour, standing menacingly in the hall against the dark oak panelling. She certainly grew to love the two nearly life-size bronze statues of Russian horses in the hall, with riders on their backs, and giant birds perched on their shoulders. When Mary was much older, she bought these statues in the sale of Rossmore furniture held by her brother William, the sixth Lord Rossmore, and had them shipped to her home in South Africa, where her grandchildren remember them standing guard outside her garden door.

There was so much else to discover and explore in the great house: stillrooms beside the kitchens, where jams and ciders were made; a vast laundry, with great vats for boiling linen, long wooden tables for folding the sheets, great tubs and washboards for scrubbing and an array of irons, heated by burning coals, of all shapes and sizes, a small army of laundry maids toiling away – and all this permanently shrouded in a haze of steam.

Each function of the house was performed by its own band of servants. It is doubtful if, as a child, Mary would have been allowed to spend much time in the kitchen, visiting the cook and the scullery maids. Children weren't encouraged to spend too much time with servants. One of the fears was that they would start to speak with a brogue – very infectious, but not approved of, except as a jokey way of talking. An English voice was essential in an Anglo-Irish family of that time.

Relations between master and servant in Ireland at this time were often cheerfully informal, but this was only half the story. In some respects the Anglo-Irish attitude to servants was the same as that to dogs and horses: fond, when they were behaving and in their place, but harsh if they stepped out of line. The staff did not all live in the house. The 1901 Census lists only six staff in the house, but that figure is artificially low because Lord and Lady

Rossmore and their family were away at the time, and their personal servants were away with them. In the 1911 Census there were seven living-in staff, and Derry and Mary were at home. By then Derry was far less well off. In the 1890s there were many more staff living on the estate – in the twenty cottages that existed then, and in the stable yard – who either worked outside or came up to the house each morning. People would also have been employed from the nearby town of Monaghan.

To work in the Castle was often a family affair. The gamekeeper's sons would be employed about the estate – in the timber yard or the garden – and later one of them would take over from his father. A favourite family of Mary's were the Mulligans. Micky Mulligan was the head gardener and Mary loved going to visit his family in their cottage on the estate. A few years before Mary's birth, the cook married the head gamekeeper, and their son Paddy McGuinness in turn became the head gamekeeper. Paddy worked on the estate from the age of twelve, and retired sixty years later. His son Owen, now over eighty, also worked on the estate for much of his life. When asked what the people of Monaghan thought of the Rossmores, Owen replied, 'I don't know why they should not be liked. They were inoffensive people.'

Mary was treated as a little princess. She was the eldest child, forgiven for being a girl as soon as her little brothers arrived, living in a vast castle on an enormous estate, and in a feudal atmosphere that lasted in Ireland much longer than it did in all but the very grandest houses in England. The boundary of the Rossmore estate was near the town, and there would hardly have been an inhabitant of Monaghan who would not have known Mary, or taken an interest in her as she was growing up. This feudal atmosphere did several things for a child in Mary's position. It gave her confidence in her standing in the world, and a strong sense of belonging: she was surrounded by *her* world and *her* people. It also gave her a certain arrogance. Mistakes would not be countenanced, respect would be of paramount importance, fools would not be suffered gladly. As she grew older Mary showed signs of all of these attitudes, but her most lasting characteristic was a strong affection for her roots – for her Irish home and her Irish background.

Curiously, if Mary thought of herself as having Irish blood in her veins, she would have been wrong. Her ancestry was part Scottish, part Dutch, part English. The Rossmores who married wives whose homes were in Ireland married Anglo-Irish women, not native Irish. The main reason for this was religion. Before Mary's grandmother Julia converted to Roman Catholicism in 1879, no Rossmore was a Catholic, and none married anyone who was not a Protestant – except, curiously, Mary's great grandfather Warner William Westenra, whose first wife, Marianne Walsh, was Catholic. The very fact of being born and living in Ireland made people think and talk of themselves as Irish, and have tremendous loyalty to the country, however foreign their roots. But although the Anglo-Irish were less inhibited and more gregarious than their counterparts across the Irish Sea, their customs, loyalties, education, tastes and manners were all influenced by their British origins. Louis MacNeice described the Anglo-Irish character as 'Nothing but an insidious bonhomie, an obsolete bravado, a way with horses.' Sean O'Faolain gave a more measured assessment, arguing that 'culturally speaking the Anglo-Irish were to create modern Irish-thinking, English-speaking, English-writing Ireland. Politically, and in the largest sense socially, they were either wicked, indifferent, or sheer failures.'

The Westenra/Rossmore family had the typically Anglo-Irish love of sport, and their upbringing produced a healthy, courageous attitude to life. Mary's family all had a remarkable degree of daring in their make-up. By the time Mary was six, or perhaps even younger, her father must have realized that she was going to be a good horsewoman. Children of her background started to ride when they were only three or four. Their first mount would be a donkey. Very soon a tiny pony would be found. Before long, they would be going out hunting on a leading rein. All this was probably the most important part of Mary's young life. Her mother Mittie had been an intrepid horsewoman, but after a severe riding accident, soon after she married Derry, she gave up hunting. Mittie's sister, always known as Doods or Doody, was a brilliant horsewoman, and continued to hunt into her eighties. She and Mary were very close, but it was Mary's father who was her main mentor and guide.

2

Derry Rossmore and Richard Naylor

Derry Westenra, born in 1853, was the second of six children of Henry Robert, the third Lord Rossmore. His elder brother, Henry Cairnes, known as 'Rosie', became the fourth Lord at the age of nine, upon the death of their father. Rosie was sent to Eton, Derry to Rugby. Derry had no expectations: all was to be Rosie's. When Derry was sixteen Rosie joined the prestigious regiment of Life Guards. Derry himself went into a less fashionable regiment, the Ninth Lancers, at nineteen.

Two years later, in 1874, everything changed. Rosie, riding in the Guards Cup Race at Winsdor Steeplechases, was mortally injured by a fall from his horse. The story is told that as he lay in agony he uttered a series of shocking curses – much to the dismay of Queen Victoria, who was in attendance. Three days later Rosie died.

Thus, at the age of twenty-one, totally unprepared, Derry became the fifth Lord Rossmore. Until then he had been enjoying life in a cheerfully feckless and irresponsible way, as recounted much later in his memoirs, *Things I Can Tell*. It is a silly book, but it is obviously the picture of himself that Derry wanted to leave to posterity, and it tells us much of what we know about him as a young man. His neighbour, Leonie Leslie, said it should have been called *Things I Should Not Tell*. Derry hoped to be seen as a devil-may-care buccaneer who took extraordinarily foolish risks, gambled, philandered, spent recklessly – and, when occasionally looking for excuses for this behaviour, blamed it all on the fact that he was 'an Irishman'.

He wrote of himself at the age of twenty-three: 'I found myself in the year I retired from the Guards the owner of a fine property and a good income. I had likewise excellent health and the Irishman's capacity to enjoy life, so it is small wonder that I threw myself into the pursuit of pleasure and determined to have a thorough good time.' This he proceeded to do, for the rest of his life – and when his own funds ran out, as they quickly did, he found means, and people with means, to finance him. His greatest gift, it would seem, was this capacity to get other people to pay his extravagant bills.

Derry certainly also had a capacity to make friends. His enthusiasm for his pursuits and pastimes was infectious. When he was a boy, it was hunting, fishing, shooting, cock-fighting and drinking. 'Those distant days were very happy ones,' he wrote. 'I used to hunt by moonlight with Dick [his brother], and as this happened after dinner, reckless riding was more likely than not.' The book is full of descriptions of drinking bouts. 'When I was a young man the Irish took their whack just as their forbears had done – we were used to rough nights.' On one such night Derry and his friends mercilessly left a man whom they felt had offended them to sink up to his neck in a bog.

Another impression Derry was happy to give was that he was a great ladies' man. He tells a story of a woman whose husband was badly injured in his private parts in a fight. Derry later encounters the wife, looking miserable. When he realizes who she is, and why she's so gloomy, he says to her, 'If I wasn't due at the meet, I'd just get off my horse and have some further conversation with you.' She replies: 'Ah – ah, I know ye now. Sure and you're Master Derry. Well well, I've always heered tell that you're an obleeging blackguard!'

He was a gambler. His younger brother once arranged a cock-fight in the kitchen of the courthouse in Monaghan, while acting as secretary to the Grand Jury. They also bet on badger-baiting. Two badgers would be let loose together, and then, Derry said, 'the fun commenced'. He tells a story of a local lawyer coming to dinner at Rossmore. After dinner they let the badgers loose with the dogs. The lawyer toppled drunkenly into the pit where the dogs and badgers were fighting. 'Joe fell right in the middle of the combatants, and, once down, he couldn't get up. All we could see was Joe's inert form with any number of dogs running over it, snapping and yapping at the badgers.' This was thought hilariously funny.

One of the few dates in his book is the year he started racing – 1878, when he was twenty-five. By then he had been lord and master of Rossmore for four years. He started on the Curragh, in Co. Kildare, and later trained at Epsom and Newmarket in England. Racing became a passion to him, and also the means of losing an enormous amount of money. He did have some successes, however. His greatest win was the City and Suburban in 1882, with his horse Passaic. This coincided with a significant interview with his future father-in-law, Richard Naylor. Derry was not able to watch his horse win, as he had elected to go that afternoon to ask for the hand of Mr Naylor's elder daughter Mittie. He describes the interview:

> I found the old man lying on the sofa … pretending to be very ill. It was then three o'clock, and as I knew that Passaic had won the race, I greeted him by saying, 'How are you? I've won the City and Suburban.' He huddled himself up and just grunted by way of an answer. Said I, 'I've come to ask you to allow me to marry your daughter; that's why I'm here.' 'Go away, Rossmore,' he replied in peevish accents. 'I tell you I'm far too ill to discuss those sorts of things.' But suddenly his sporting instincts overcame his grumpiness, and he jumped up like a two-year-old, saying, as he did so, 'But have you *really* won the City and Suburban?'

Naylor was an extraordinarily wealthy man. The house in which that interview took place was Downshire House, his London residence, in Belgrave Square. He was for a time the Master of the Pytchley hunt in Northamptonshire – an influential position. Naylor had two eligible daughters. Derry wrote of him: 'He hated the Irish "like fun": in truth, he detested most men and especially those that came after his girls. Personally I don't believe he really minded whether they got married or not: it was merely his dislike of "forking out" the settlement money which made him so loth to part with his daughters.' And this is the crux of the matter. Naylor was probably aware that the most attractive thing about his daughters was the money they would get from him when they married. He was likely to be extremely suspicious of any young man coming after them, particularly a young rake-about-town like Derry. He was also, as Derry claimed, prejudiced against the Irish. At the height of the Great Famine in Ireland in the late 1840s, Naylor sent a boat over to Ireland, filled it to the brim with unemployed labourers, and sailed it back to Liverpool, thereby hoping to equip himself with cheap labour, while giving the workers the means to eat. But the scheme failed: the men, for whatever reason, wouldn't work for him. Naylor shipped the workers back to Ireland and vowed to have as little as possible to do with the Irish from then on.

Derry claimed that 'it didn't matter to me if Mittie Naylor hadn't a penny in the world: I was in love with her, and we determined to get married whenever the opportunity presented itself'. This suggests there was some strong opposition. The opportunity only presented itself when she reached twenty-one, and was free to make her own decisions. Her father's opposition to the match would have made it much more dramatic and exciting for her. Derry was, in her eyes, a romantic character: a young peer (whereas Naylor was a commoner whose family had come to prominence through trade and banking); the owner of a grand castle in Ireland; a dashing, courageous, good-looking fellow who moved in the highest society; a former officer in the Brigade of Guards; a man with an inherited position of influence in his own county – all this, and, as well, he was fun to be with, flirtatious, outrageous, a bit of a risk, and not at all boring to a girl who had been brought up to respect horses and hunting as greatly superior to books and learning. She was dazzled by the outward show of the man, and he did everything he could to foster her image of him as a man who would dare all to capture her.

To have persuaded Mittie to be his wife was a great achievement for Derry, and whatever he might have said about it not mattering to him whether or not Mittie had a penny in the world, he was certainly the one man in the world who needed a rich wife. Years later Mittie was to say, 'All I ever seem to do is write cheques.' In *Things I Can Tell*, apart from his encounter with her father, Derry scarcely mentions Mittie, except to explain that she gave up hunting after a serious fall which concussed her for several hours. He writes of his daughter Mary only once, and of his sons not at all, except, on the final page, to say, 'I am fortunate in possessing a charming wife and the best children in the world.'

Richard Naylor, when he looked so glum the afternoon Derry came to call, had assessed the situation accurately. Derry was a spendthrift, and needed a large supply of ready cash. At the time of Derry's wedding, Naylor was one of many people known popularly as 'the richest commoner in England'. As the years went on, his relationship with Derry went from bad to worse.

Richard Naylor founded his racing stud at Hooton in the 1850s, proposing to race on a big scale. Hooton was close to the Marquis of Westminster's stud at Eaton Hall, and in 1860 Naylor bought six of Lord Westminster's yearlings. One of these became his most famous and successful racer, Macaroni, who won the Derby in 1863. Naylor cleared nearly £100,000 by backing Macaroni when he stood at 50 to 1 to win at Epsom.

After three years of racing, Naylor put Macaroni to stud at Hooton, and soon after that he added to his stud the most famous stallion of all time: Stockwell. Naylor bought the horse at the end of his racing career in order to breed from him. The fee for Macaroni's services was thirty guineas. At the date of the stallion's death no fewer than ninety-two of his daughters were included in the stud-book.

Hunting was Naylor's other great passion. In order to hunt with the Pytchley, he bought Kelmarsh Hall in Northamptonshire in 1875. He did not embellish Kelmarsh, a fine Georgian house, with Victorian elaborations, apart from building on a ballroom and importing a lot of ugly Italian marble for the chapel. (In 1891 Mary Westenra was christened there, as a baby of two months – Richard Naylor's first grandchild.) The Prince of Wales would have hunted with the Pytchley, and probably stayed at Kelmarsh. He was certainly a friend of the Naylor daughters, Mittie and Doods. (In 1890 Doods was a guest in the house party at Tranby Croft at the time of the notorious cheating scandal at the game of cards in which the Prince of Wales was playing.)

Kelmarsh Hall was 'the house on the hill', a classical Palladian villa designed by the great architect James Gibbs, who was responsible for St Martin-in-the-Fields in Trafalgar Square and the marvellous Gibbs building in King's College, Cambridge. The house was sold in 1908, when Mary was seventeen.

Richard Naylor was of his time: a man who wished to impress the world with the size of his fortune. Hooton Hall was a perfect counterpart to Rossmore Castle. Before Naylor bought Hooton in 1848 and laid his enlarging hand on it, it was a respectable square-fronted Georgian mansion. He proceeded to make it into a palace. Long wings were built on either side of the main block; a chapel was incorporated into one, and a vast sculpture gallery into the other. A great tower with a cupola on top embellished the skyline. Urns and statues were liberally scattered along the top of the new balustrades around the roof, and pillared porticoes added to the front garden.

All this work by Mary's grandfather Naylor was being carried out at the same time as her grandfather Rossmore was enlarging Rossmore Castle, on an equally extravagant scale. Why did they do it? Was it simply to show off their wealth and importance? Rossmore Castle was poorly and cheaply constructed. The money was not there to make a long-lasting job, and less than a hundred years later the castle had to be pulled down. Hooton Hall was eventually destroyed too, but for a different reason. It was used to house the R.A.F. during the Second World War, and was left in a bad state. The Air Ministry sold off some of the land, and an enormous Vauxhall car factory was built in the grounds. It had been left to Derry Rossmore's son Richard, rather than to his elder son William, who became the sixth Lord Rossmore, because by then Richard Naylor had become so sick of Derry's extravagances that he vowed that not a penny more of his would go to financing the Rossmore estate. Hooton Hall was pulled down in 1946. Rossmore Castle was pulled down in – 1946. Less than a hundred years of splendour – and in the midst of that extravagance the child Mary Westenra was born, at a time when it must have seemed to her grandparents and parents that their dynasties were set to continue for centuries.

3

Derry and Mittie

When Derry Rossmore married Mittie Naylor in 1882 he bore her back to his romantic castle deep in the bogs of Ireland. It would be fascinating to know how she reacted as she arrived at Monaghan station, to be greeted as her daughter Mary would be twenty-eight years later, after her marriage to Abe Bailey. Mittie was the young, handsome, wealthy bride of the great landlord of Monaghan; the chatelaine-to-be; the employer of a vast army of outdoor and indoor servants; the wife of the man to whom the rents of the town were paid.

Having been brought up by Richard Naylor, Mittie would have had her own ideas about how large houses should be run. Derry's mother, the redoubtable Julia, who was left a widow with six small children but who nevertheless was able to persuade George Stacpoole to become her second husband, must have been relieved to see the rich young heiress appear, and to realize that the burden of running Rossmore on a shoestring was to be lifted from her shoulders.

Derry held a title which probably meant nothing at all to Mittie: he was the County Grand Master of the Loyal Orange Order of County Monaghan. It was in this capacity that, in the year after his marriage, Derry achieved his greatest moment of fame. The Orange Order had been founded in County Armagh in 1795, a time when loyal Protestantism felt itself under threat from the Catholic 'Defenders' and the United Irishmen, who opposed being ruled from England. The men who founded the Order wanted to ban

Catholics from the local linen industry, and they wanted to keep in with the Protestant ascendancy, who were their landlords. Baron Smith, in 1813, described the attitude of Orangemen as 'a spurious and illiberal loyalty which grows up amongst the vulgar classes, and which is very turbulent, bigoted, riotous and affronting, very saucy, and overbearing, almost proud of transgression, necessarily producing exasperation, and often leading to the effusion of blood'.

The Baron's remark about 'the vulgar classes' notwithstanding, and in spite of his father's and grandfather's support for Catholic Emancipation and O'Connell, Derry Rossmore did not think it odd, in the early days of his manhood, that he should be the figurehead in Monaghan for such an organization. In the Ulster border counties the Protestant ascendancy believed it their duty to give a responsible lead to their tenantry. It was thought very important that the Protestant influence should be paramount, and Orangeism was one means of ensuring this. Derry probably didn't think much about the significance of being the County Grand Master. It is possible that the position went with his title as Lord Rossmore.

Derry's great day came in 1883. The nationalist leader Charles Stewart Parnell, at the height of his power, had announced a meeting to be held in a field outside Rosslea in Co. Fermanagh, on 16 October. Derry Rossmore, together with a Mr J. Wallace Taylor, issued a counter-proclamation. Derry was its author. It read:

> The late Invincibles and Land Leaguers are afraid to enter Monaghan, but they have flooded your county with proclamations asking your attendance at Rosslea on 16th October, to hear their treasonable speeches.
>
> Attend there, with Sir John Leslie, Colonel Lloyd and myself, to assist our Fermanagh brethren in supporting their rights, and oppose the rebels to the utmost, showing them that the Orangemen are, as heretofore, loyal to England. They declare that you are as ready to obey them as their dupes in the south, but we will show them, as did the Tyrone men, that they are liars and slanderers. Boycott and Emergency men to the front, and down with Parnell and rebellion! God Save the Queen!

He inspired 3000 Monaghan men, who were joined by 4000 Fermanagh men and another 1000 men on the road, to march to the field adjoining the one in which the Parnellites – over 3000 of them – had assembled. On the way they were confronted by the Resident Magistrate, a Captain McTernon, who attempted to prevent the Orangemen from continuing. Derry refused to give ground, asking the R.M. if he had any authority to prevent them from using that road; the R.M. had to say that he had none. McTernon said later that bad language and threats had been used by Lord Rossmore's companions, but not by his lordship himself. So, despite his protests, the vast march continued on its way. Derry later explained in his book that the two fields were separated by a stream with a bridge across it, and that it was obvious to any fool that the bridge could easily be defended by only two men, so there was no danger of its being crossed. The chair at the Orange meeting was taken by Viscount Crichton, the eldest son of the Earl of Erne, of Crum Castle, Co. Fermanagh, and the resolution was proposed by Lord Rossmore, that Orangemen 'solemnly bind ourselves to maintain the union between Great Britain and Ireland, and resist in every way and by all means, any attempt to place Ireland under a government of murderers, butchers, and socialistic rebels'.

The R.M. asked Derry not to march back along the same route. Derry knew his followers would think this a capitulation, but he eventually agreed, and (according to his book) made a speech to the assembled throng telling them that, if they disobeyed, and went back the way they came, 'You shall only do so over my body.' They did as he asked, with no further trouble.

Amazingly, the whole incident passed off in a peaceful manner, and the day became a personal triumph for Derry, who was asked to address meetings and attend rallies all over the north of Ireland. When he went by train to Belfast, at every stop on the way there were crowds waiting to cheer him, and he addressed them from the steps of his carriage. Shane Leslie, in his book *The Film of Memory*, wrote: 'Had Rossmore possessed any eloquence, he could have seized the leadership of Ulster at that fervid moment.'

Derry's foolhardy Orange outing had one or two unfortunate results. The Resident Magistrate was angry that his authority had been flouted. A complaint was made to the secretary of the Lords Commissioners for the Custody of the Great Seal of Ireland, and Lord Rossmore was told he would be removed from his position as Her Majesty's Commissioner of the Peace. Even after receiving several letters of explanation as to his actions, the secretary was adamant that Derry should be deprived of this office. J. Wallace Taylor, his co-marcher, wrote a book called *The Rossmore Incident* in which he provided a list of all the magistrates in different counties of Ireland – titled aristocrats, mostly – who wrote to declare their support for Derry in his actions, and their disapproval of his demotion. Despite this support, Derry was not reinstated as a magistrate for several years.

We can only guess at the life Derry and Mittie lived in these early years of their marriage. The pattern of their year was clearly defined. From August to March they were in Ireland. From April to July they were in England: in London for the season, which lasted from May to the end of June, and at Cowes week, which would have been important to them, as Derry's father had owned large yachts. Race meetings, and house parties in different parts of England with the Prince of Wales's set, filled up more spaces in their social diaries. Derry's book is filled with stories about the Prince, whom he often met at the races.

There are theories among Mittie's descendants that she was a much closer friend of the man who was to become Edward VII than her husband was. Hints have even been made that she might have been his lover – and that her first child, Mary, might have been his.

Mary's eldest daughter, Mary Ellen, believed that Mary knew of her mother's sexual adventures, which shocked her to the extent of making her almost paranoically prudish about all things to do with sex in her own and her children's lives. This side of the family believes that Mittie slept with the Prince of Wales.

None of Mittie's children resembled each other – feeding the view that they may have had three different fathers – and none inherited Derry's stammer, which he claimed was a family trait. Some descendants believe that Derry was 'too drunk' to perform his marital duties, and that this forced Mittie, after eight years of trying and failing to produce an heir, to turn elsewhere. This seems an unlikely explanation, however, as Derry was known to have several mistresses. Desmond Leslie said Derry 'kept a French lady in Portadown. You see, you could hop on a train, it was only five stops up the line, about half an hour'. Desmond's father, Sir Shane, said of her, 'The poor lady looked at the rain every day, falling on the Orange parade, and she died of ennui.'

Although it is likely that both Derry and Mittie had extramarital affairs, there is no evidence, beyond family tattle (perhaps born of wishful thinking), that Mittie had an affair with the Prince of Wales. There is some circumstantial evidence to the contrary. In 1889, the year before Mary was born, the Prince had fallen madly in love with Daisy Brooke, the wife of the future Earl of Warwick. He spent the next six years of his life ensnared by her charms, and even after the affair became platonic, he was her devoted slave. He wrote to her in 1897: 'How could you, my loved one, imagine that I should withdraw my friendship with you? On the contrary, I want to befriend you more than ever ... my own lovely little Daisy [my wife] really forgives and condones the past as I have corroborated what you wrote about our friendship having been platonic for some years.'

Mittie's life can't have been easy, complicated as it was by her father's contempt for Derry, and her position as go-between, continually having to provide her father's money for her husband's profligate ways. Alcohol and infidelity would only have made things worse. It was into this complex relationship that Mary was born, on 1 December 1890.

4

Mary's Childhood

In spite of the underlying troubles of her parents' lives, Mary looked back on her childhood as idyllic, and this was because of the magic of Rossmore. As she grew up in her enchanted castle, surrounded by the towering woods and the lakes of the estate, where she was free, yet safe, there can't have been much her childish heart desired that was denied her. This was why for Mary, in later life (spent mostly in England and South Africa), everything Irish was good. Ireland – Rossmore – was a place where, from the perspective of older, sadder times, it seemed she had always been happy.

Her relationship with her father was always good, that with her mother much less so. She and Derry shared a love of horses, outdoor sports and high-speed exploits. Mittie had given up hunting before Mary was born, and she might have felt twinges of jealousy as she watched her husband and daughter so rapturously enjoying a sport she had once loved so much herself.

Hunting was Mary's passion from an early age. In Monaghan there had existed a pack of hounds known as the Monaghan Harriers – which meant that their quarry was not foxes, but hares. It was disbanded for several years, but in 1904 there appeared a notice in the local paper, the *Northern Standard*: 'A meeting will be held in the Westenra Arms on Monday next at 12.0 to take into consideration the possibilities of re-starting the Monaghan Harriers for the coming winter. Those interested in the matter are requested to be present.'

The Westenra Arms, a hotel in the centre of Monaghan, just beside a memorial to Mary's uncle Rosie, belonged to Derry. Probably it was at his instigation that the meeting was held. Certainly he would have been there, and so would Mary, aged thirteen. Derry and Mary were to be seen at almost every meet of the Monaghan Harriers from then on, the first meet being on 5 November 1904, three weeks before Mary's fourteenth birthday. She was out hunting all through the winter of 1905, which shows that she was not away at boarding school, but being educated at home during that winter.

Mary did attend Heathfield School, Ascot, for one disastrous term in 1906; she hated it so much that she ran away, and she was not made to go back. The one event we know about from her time at Heathfield was that she was confirmed in Holy Trinity Church, Bracknell, on 18 November 1906, just before her sixteenth birthday.

A girls' boarding school, however well run, however fashionable, must have seemed a prison to a child whose instincts were all for adventure. To run away takes initiative and courage, a paradox summed up by T.S. Eliot in his play *The Family Reunion*:

> In a world of fugitives
> The person taking the opposite direction
> Will appear to run away.

Mary was allowed to return to her horses and her hunting, and was taught by two remarkable sisters from Russia, who came to Rossmore and continued her education there. Alma and Yelma Hemmerlé came from an aristocratic Franco-Russian background. Mary must have become very fond of the sisters, because years later she was still in touch with them and both her son and grandson remember meeting them. Through them she learned to speak good French. Although she is not remembered now as being particularly intellectual, she was well educated by the two Misses Hemmerlé, and books of hers, annotated in her own handwriting, show that her reading was eclectic and intelligent.

But Mary was basically an outdoor child. Before the Monaghan Harriers were re-established, she took part on horseback in the Monaghan County Show, which took place every September on the Rossmore estate. The year before, in 1903, when Mary was twelve, her father had constructed a new jumping enclosure in Rossmore Park, and it was inaugurated on 10 September 1903, with displays of driving and horse jumping and tug-of-war competitions, accompanied by the band of the Third Battalion of the Irish Fusiliers. Admission was sixpence, with 1*s*. 6*d*. extra for the grandstand enclosure. Mary performed sidesaddle, as she always rode, on one of her favourite horses. In 1907 Mary and her father both competed in the Monaghan County Show. Mary won third prize in the jumping competition on her horse Tullaghan, and Derry won first prize in the Monaghan Harriers competition.

A picture of Mary, looking most charming and feminine in a wide-brimmed flowery hat and diaphanous accordion-pleated dress, appeared in the *Irish Society and Social Review* of 13 March 1909. The picture was accompanied by a description of Mary as

> a girl who is very cheery and bright, who loves dancing and music. She is voted 'a real good sort' among her friends. She has a good seat riding, good hands, and can put a horse well at a fence and gallop it across a field. She has had a fair amount of hunting with her aunt, Miss Naylor, and among hunting people that will speak for itself. She has a 20 bore shotgun with which she is making rapid progress towards becoming a good shot, and is very keen on the sport. She is fond of all games, such as lawn tennis, golf etc. (BUT) She has been doing too much lately, and has in consequence been on the sick list, and has been told she must 'go slow' for a year.

There is no evidence that she 'went slow'. Just before her nineteenth birthday Mary achieved the remarkable distinction of being elected to the Mastership of the Monaghan Harriers. There must have been very few Masters anywhere in these islands who were only eighteen, and even fewer who were eighteen and female. It was a terrific achievement, and says a great deal about her character. She was not particularly imposing to look at, being only five foot four, slight and feminine looking, with a lithe figure. But her appearance was deceptive. Already she was renowned for a delight in taking risks. She is still famous in that part of the world for having jumped the fearsome 'Double Jump at Magheranny'.

An announcement in the *Northern Standard* of 19 December 1909 read:

> The meeting of the Monaghan Harriers on Saturday was at Summerhill, and the new Master, the Hon. Mary Westenra, was enabled for the first time to take up her position. Miss Westenra was up till a week ago in London, in attendance on her mother, who was suffering from indisposition, but her ladyship is now happily recovering. Miss Westenra was cordially welcomed on Saturday ... the remarkable feature of the meeting was the number of dogs present.

On 24 December 1909, the following notice appeared: 'The meets of the Monaghan harriers will be on 24th and 27th December. Gentlemen and Ladies are particularly requested not to ride over any young grass or seeds. Mary Westenra, Master.' What was unusual about this announcement was that up until then the notice had always been addressed only to 'Gentlemen', although Mary was not the only woman out hunting. A more feminist attitude had arrived.

Mary was a courageous point-to-point rider. On 6 April 1910 she rode in the first race at Tullaghan. There were eleven horses, five of them ridden by ladies. During the race Mary bore to the right, with others, consequently going wide of the course. On 5 April 1911 Mary was again riding in the local point-to-point. In the Ladies' race she led up to the last jump, when her mount Jamieson stumbled, and finished third.

Her aunt Doods was reputed to be the finest horsewoman in the hunting field of her day. She owned a large house, Knossington, near Kelmarsh, in Rutlandshire. She hunted until she was eighty, and was always a great friend to Mary, and a tremendous influence.

Mary got on with her much better than with her own mother. She and Doods were both good at drawing, and sent each other letters full of the most malicious and delightful cartoons of their various unfortunate friends out hunting. Mary kept these in several scrapbooks and they clearly show her sense of humour and her pleasure in poking fun at the misfortunes of others. She also painted in watercolours.

Mary was also passionate about dogs, and photographs from her childhood show her surrounded by them. A type of setter, known as the Rossmore setter, was bred for many generations on the estate. A photograph of Mary taken by her brother William when she was fifteen shows her with an assortment of dogs – a springer spaniel, a fox terrier, what might be a cairn. There is also a photograph of her with her father, taken in 1908, with an enormous Irish wolfhound dwarfing the two of them as she perches on the arm of her father's chair in the library at Rossmore. Mary has not yet got her hair 'up', which shows she has not yet 'come out'. This great event was due to happen when she was eighteen, and involved her presentation at court in London as a debutante. After this watershed, young girls were considered to be grown up enough to join their parents' social events, and were also expected to find eligible and wealthy husbands.

Edward VII was still on the throne when Mary was presented in 1909. There is a formal portrait photograph of her taken after this event, with her hair piled up precariously over her ears, a bejewelled bodice, and a swathe of satin falling down from her slim waist. It doesn't show the ostrich feathers that she would have worn in her hair, or her fan, or her train. Her hairstyle makes her look older than eighteen, and she has a severe, almost disapproving expression on her face. This formality was not natural to her: she was much happier hacking about the fields and hills of Monaghan on her beloved Tullaghan.

Her 'Season' in London, however, had to be endured. All the many balls, given by the mothers of her fellow debutantes, had to be attended. Her own ball, given by her mother in a house, probably rented for the season, in Lowndes Square, was talked about in Monaghan for years afterwards. Another ball which Mary attended, because of her mother's friendship with the King, was the evening party at Buckingham Palace on 9 July 1909. Seventeen hundred guests were invited. However much Mary longed for her Monaghan hills, she must have loved the splendour of that evening.

At various moments in her childhood Mary must have been aware of the problems in her parents' lives. A persistent problem was Derry's extravagant spending on entertainment and on grandiose 'improvements' to the estate, such as the digging of five new lakes.

Derry's drinking, which fed a violent temper, was a source of unhappiness to Mittie and, perhaps, to Mary. Her abhorrence for alcohol as an adult may have been a reaction against Derry's abuse of it, while her own appalling temper was an inheritance she never mastered. Derry's substantial position in local society may have been a further source of anxiety. In 1904 Derry drew the wrath of the Protestant press by resigning as County Grand Master of the Orange Order. He had been influenced by a movement in Ireland, of which the figurehead was the Earl of Dunraven, which was pressing for devolution of certain powers from Britain to Ireland. This smacked to loyal Orangemen of a longing for Home Rule. Derry was moved to write a somewhat intemperate letter to the local Orangemen, which was published in the local paper. He had decided that 'Local Orangeism was coming to mean an organisation seeking to establish the worst mental slavery – that their attitude is solely negative, ever in opposition, ever seeking to sow dissension.'

This caused an uproar, and some of his neighbours and friends, who still belonged to the Orange Order, such as the Earl of Erne and the Maddens, castigated him. It must have been a confusing time for the children, who knew themselves to be part of the Protestant Ascendancy tradition, which had been linked with Orangeism for over a hundred years, and which meant to them Orange parades on the Twelfth of July, when Derry would appear in his full regalia of orange sash and bowler hat and white gloves, and march at the head of the noisy procession of pipes and drums to the meeting in 'The Field'. Now suddenly he had resigned, and was being treated with rage and contempt by all the Protestants in the area. Luckily, in some respects, for Mary and her brothers, the majority of people of Monaghan were Catholic and nationalist, and therefore delighted at Derry's defection. But most of Mary's close friends and their parents would have been appalled, and she must have suffered. The incident might have given her, at thirteen, a deeper understanding of the conflicts at the core of Irish life.

One of Derry's excuses for leaving the Orange Order was that he was Lord Lieutenant of the county of Monaghan. This meant that he was the Sovereign's representative in the county, and was therefore supposed to be non-political. He continued as Lord Lieutenant for many years, and whenever he got the chance he made loyal speeches for King Edward and Queen Alexandra, to show that even though no longer an Orangeman he was thoroughly loyal to the Crown.

In 1908 Derry caused a new furore in the neighbourhood – one which Mary must have adored. He bought a motor car, said to be the first to appear in the county. It was probably manufactured in Belfast, where some of the earliest cars were made. Derry employed a chauffeur, but loved to drive it himself. Desmond Leslie remembers that the car

> had venetian blinds, which used to come off with a huge clatter if you took the corners too fast, and the estate carpenter would have to put them on again. It was the terror of the county. They used to drive up to their shooting lodge at Eshnaglough, in the Bragan hills, and old Derry never knew when to change gear, so the gamekeeper, who could drive the car, had to stick up little signposts, all the way to Eshnaglough from Rossmore, about fifteen miles, with 1, 2, 3 on them, which told Lord Rossmore which gear to be in. Once he banged it into reverse by mistake, and there was this terrible clatter as all the venetian blinds flew off.

Perhaps inspired by her father's automobile, Mary bought herself a motor bike. The passion for speed and danger was part of her psyche, and in Monaghan the fastest and most daring thing, after her hunters, was this newfangled machine that roared along noisily, scattering people, dogs, donkey carts and babies in prams in its fumey wake.

Mary also had a gun. She was invited to Castle Leslie in November 1908, to join a large house-party which involved three days of pheasant-shooting. It was unusual in those days for women to take part in such a masculine sport. They would go out with the guns, but were meant to stand behind somewhere, watching admiringly and murmuring 'Good shot, darling' when their better halves achieved a right and left. This wouldn't do for Mary. She had a masculine streak, and needed to be out at the forefront of things.

The Rossmores had their own idiosyncratic method of fishing on their numerous lakes, which were well stocked with fish. They had specially constructed rafts, made of wood and reeds, on which they stood in the middle of the lake. Mary and her brothers all became expert at catching fish in this manner.

She grew up among a circle of people who lived in the same way as her parents – in large houses on big estates – and her friends, from childhood through adolescence, were the children of these neighbouring families. The Alexanders, living nearby in Caledon, Co. Tyrone, were one such family. Harold Alexander, the second son, later the celebrated Field Marshal, was a year younger than Mary, and he and she were extremely close friends. They wrote to each other constantly throughout their formative years. Mary was really fond of him, and would probably have liked to marry him, but her father and mother had other ideas for her, which involved someone who had better prospects than a younger son, and a lot more money. Years later, Mary's niece Brigid Westenra was staying at Government House in Canada when Lord Alexander was the Governor General. She remembers being surprised that he was so particularly kind to her, persuading her to stay on long after she had meant to leave. When she told him she wasn't sure in which direction her life should go next, he suggested she should learn to fly, which she did. She did not know of his previous close friendship with her Aunt Mary, but when told of it, she suddenly understood why he had taken such a friendly interest in her.

Mary's life between her coming out in London and her engagement to Abe Bailey when she was twenty was typical of the life lived by young girls of her background before the First World War. Aged eighteen and nineteen, with sociable parents and masses of contacts all over England and Ireland and Scotland, her life was filled with all the things she enjoyed most: hunting, shooting, staying away in weekend house-parties, race meetings, balls, formal receptions in Dublin Castle and Buckingham Palace. An account in the magazine *Black and White*, dated 11 December 1909, gives a vivid impression of what her life was like at that time:

> As an instance of the keenness of the modern sportswoman, I think a three days record by the Hon. Mary Westenra, Master of the Monaghan Harriers, is worth recording: (1) a hard day with the Pytchley; changed, and dined at her Aunt's house in Market Harborough; then travelled all night to her home at Rossmore in Ireland. (2) Having breakfasted, hunted all day with the Monaghan Harriers. (3) Had a horse running in each of the three point-to-point races: won all three!

On 2 August 1911, Mary was staying at a house called Thornhill, West Cowes, in the Isle of Wight. The day before she had been a guest of Lord Iveagh, on his yacht. She had news for her younger brother Richard:

> Dear Dick,
> How are you getting on? – I have news to tell you but perhaps you have heard it from Daddy: but at present it is an *absolute secret* to be told to *no-one* – I am engaged to be married to Sir Abe Bailey – a man of 46 – a widower with two children – a boy of 11 and a girl of – I don't know a bit older I imagine–!!! I suppose you will laugh – we are going out to South Africa on the second of September and going to stay at his 2 places out there and then at Cape Town and then go to the Durbar[?] and then I don't know if he will come back here again from that or not – I am trying to get a maid who

will travel – Brown and I went and got up at 5.30 this morning and went bathing and she wouldn't bathe she stood on the shore and watched – the tide went down very strong and coming back against it I couldn't get on at all so I didn't swim out at all only just swam up and down the shore – we went sailing on Lord Iveagh's yacht yesterday – racing and a man up aloft cut the rope he was hanging on to up in the cross-trees and fell straight down into the sea: luckily for him the boat was leaning over terrifically on one side or else he would have fallen onto the deck and there would have been an end of him altogether but a man got hold of his foot and then the crew or some of them got ahold of his leg and finally pulled him out but he had caught the … (I don't know what you call them but its what the ropes are onto outside the bulwarks) as he bent down which broke his fall; so they gave him a lot of brandy and he then said that the sea was wonderfully warm!!! And he was an old man too but bar bruises I think he was alright, but it was pretty lucky as he came from a good height as the Zitona weighs 300 tons so she isn't small – no more time now, I must change as I am going to breakfast and sail with Mrs Ernest Guinness on their yacht today – this afternoon we play tennis – the Nevada Cyril's yacht in same race and yesterday broke its mast in two places and had to be towed back – a great disappointment to all on board – Best love. Your loving Mary.

Love to Daddy – How are the dogs.

The strong impression the letter gives is that the event of the man falling from the masthead was much more exciting than her own engagement. It seems the letter of a child – a very energetic one – who got up at 5.30 to swim, then wrote to her brother, then went out to breakfast and to sail, and in the afternoon was going to play tennis. It was this sort of unbounded energy that stood her in such good stead when she took on her marathon flights across Africa in later life. In the event, she did not get married until 5 September – just over a month after the letter, and three days after the date on which they had originally planned to sail, as husband and wife, to

South Africa. Still, it was a hurried engagement, which led on to a marriage that lasted until Abe Bailey's death, twenty-nine years later.

5

Abe Bailey

Abe Bailey was once prompted to say, in front of an illustrious gathering of the mighty and great banqueting at the Mansion House in London, that he was where he was and who he was entirely through his unaided tugging at his own bootstraps.

'I did not come out of the top drawer,' he said. 'I am the son of emigrants: I love South Africa with all my heart, for it was there that I was able to rise from the bottom of the ladder.'

This was bluntly spoken. In an age and society when background and breeding seemed of the utmost importance, it was bravely spoken. His father, Thomas, was indeed an emigrant to South Africa. He had come from The Manor House, Keighley, Yorkshire in the late 1850s, with his Scottish-born wife Ann Drummond, and, by the time Abe was born on 6 November 1864, had established his own business as a general dealer in the town of Cradock, on the edge of the Karoo.

And while Abe was over-egging the pudding a little when he spoke of having been at 'the bottom of the ladder', it is true that he rejected the comfortable option of sheltering under his father's wing. Thomas Bailey's success led to a move to Queenstown, where he set up a larger business and later became mayor, and an M.P. in the Cape parliament. Abe could easily have become a similarly worthy well-to-do small-town citizen like his father. But he was born a rebel.

Not many children at the age of seven succeed in running away from home and staying away for nearly a year, but Abe did. He was one of three children: the only son, with two sisters (to whom he remained close all his life). When he was seven his mother died, and already his relationship with his father was bad. He ran to the house of an Afrikaner family not far from Queenstown, and there he stayed, happy in the house of a kind mother figure and protected from a father with whom he was perpetually at loggerheads. In this house Abe discovered a different side of South Africa. He became familiar with the Dutch antecedents which were the background to the Afrikaner way of life, and he learned to speak Afrikaans, which was extremely useful to him in later years. Combined with his love of his own British culture this Afrikaner influence led him to be known later on as 'the complete South African'.

Before the year was out, this headstrong boy was hauled back to his family home, and then almost immediately sent to England, to be educated in a no-nonsense grammar school in Keighley, his father's old home in Yorkshire. There he had to walk two miles to school and back, sometimes twice a day. The education was basic and sound, and included excellent grounding in commercial subjects. From there he was sent to Clewer House School in Windsor, Berkshire. This was a private school, which called itself a 'Classical and Commercial Academy' and catered to the sons of tradesmen and shopkeepers. Although Abe, unlike most of his classmates, did not go on to join his father's business, the school had a most profound effect on him – so much so that throughout his life he called his businesses, his farms, his houses, even his yachts, by the name of Clewer, and his son Jim has carried on the tradition. Abe stayed at Clewer House for three years, until he was fifteen. He was impatient to be out in the world, learning from doing, and not from a blackboard.

His father suggested he should go to university. Abe was not interested. Later in his life he said of himself: 'I longed to come to grips with tougher and thornier problems than either Keighley or Clewer could set me. I felt like a boxer who had had enough of sparring and wanted to get right into the ring, to square up to somebody who had got to be knocked out.' It was an apt simile for Abe: it encapsulated his pugnacious character, and he did in fact become a boxer – a very good one, winning the amateur middleweight championship of South Africa as a young man.

So, at fifteen, Abe found himself a job in the City of London, with Spreckley White and Levis, a textile firm. His father might have thought this an encouraging sign: much of his own business was wool. He naturally expected that Abe would come back to South Africa and help him, and experience with a firm of wool-buyers would be useful. But before he was seventeen, Abe had realized that the sort of life he wanted to lead was not to be found in the tradition-bound City. While he was there, however, he fell under the spell of an extraordinary and charismatic character, General Bramwell Booth, son of the founder of the Salvation Army. Because of this, he found himself teaching Sunday School at the old Sermon Lane Mission in the East End. He said of Booth: 'He was no mere pulpit Christian, he was a Christian in action, a man brimming over with pluck.' He admired the way Booth went into poverty-stricken homes where 'the devil, dirt and disease held suffering humanity in their festering grip'. He also admired the way none of Booth's preachers used notes when they spoke, and resolved that when the time came, he would do the same. Fifty years on, when he had been a member of three parliaments and addressed countless meetings, he was able to say that he had never used a note of any sort while speaking.

Abe knew that his native South Africa was a place where a man of enterprise and courage could carve out a career for himself, and he decided, aged almost seventeen, to go back. He returned to find that in the nine years he had been away his father's business had grown and prospered, and he attempted for a short time to work with him. Abe stuck at it until he was twenty-one; then, through a chance meeting with a man who had been working on the alluvial gold-fields at Pilgrim's Rest in the Transvaal, he heard of a new strike of gold at the Sheba mine in Barbertonl. The idea excited him. He had found his father's caution in business frustrating: he knew he had to break out on his own. He sold up all his possessions, and with the small amount of money this brought, set off by coach and train to Kimberley.

Abe's father had wanted him as a business partner, and after

Abe left he refused to help him financially. At one crucial point, soon after he had arrived in Barberton, when Abe was destitute, he wrote a draft on his father's name for £250. His father refused to honour it, and Abe realized he was entirely on his own.

To get to Barberton from Kimberley Abe had to endure an eight-day journey by mule-wagon, via the Witwatersrand, where the great gold-rush was underway. He had no money and the squalor, dirt and disorder of the place did not appeal to him. When he arrived at Barberton, after a futher appalling journey, he found it too was a tough, horrible place, infested by fleas and mosquitoes and every other sort of flying, biting insect. Gold-mining itself didn't appeal to him. He disliked the actual physical task of prospecting. He found he couldn't manage the pit donkeys – no doubt his short-fused temper didn't help – and he found nothing. Bored and frustrated by the whole exercise, he almost gave up altogether, contemplating working his passage to Australia. Then he decided as a last resort to try his hand at stockbroking, and borrowed £10 from a friend, Bob Bertram. (In later life Abe remembered this and repaid Bob Bertram many times over, whenever he was in financial trouble.) With this he took out a broker's licence, bought the necessary books, hung a notice on his shack saying 'Abe Bailey, Claims Broker', and with fourteen shillings in his pocket went out to drum up business.

Abe's shrewdness, persistence and courage paid dividends almost at once. His ability to speak Afrikaans was also an asset. Quite soon he was getting business from the big mining houses, including Alfred Beit and Sigismund Neumann. Alfred Graumann, who later became Mayor of Cape Town, was one of his earliest clients. He said of Abe: 'My firm gave him his first business on the local stock exchange. I saw a lot of him, and he did a great deal of business for me. Among a number of men who had their heads screwed on the right way he certainly was an outstanding youngster. I cheerfully admit he was much cleverer than I was.'

Even at his most penniless Abe was not without resources. He had been provided with a decent education; he had had experience working in a business firm in London; and he had worked for some years in his father's firm. He already had a well-trained business intelligence: he had been dealing with financial matters from the age of fifteen. All this stood him in good stead and was partly the reason why he so quickly found his feet in the stockbroking world. Nevertheless his progress wasn't all upwards: after amassing £10,000 he managed to lose it all by speculating on his own behalf. At one stage he was back to owning exactly £3. And he started again.

While this was going on he was doing other extraordinary things. He rode a horse in a circus ring, standing on its back without saddle or bridle. He won £144 17s. 6d. playing cricket for Transvaal against Natal, by a devastating display of spin bowling. He made money by boxing, having established his prowess by knocking out the landlord of the first hotel he stayed in – an experienced amateur champion. He had quickly become a well-known character in Barberton.

In 1887 Abe decided that Barberton was no longer the place for him, and went back to the Witwatersrand gold-fields, which by then had become the embryo town of Johannesburg, a settlement of tin shanties, with a few brick buildings, ugly, dreary and dirty. But it was here that Abe's fortunes began their steady rise. He took with him from Barberton his reputation for exceptional business acumen, and was therefore immediately able to borrow £4000 to make his fresh start. Many of his friends and business associates from Barberton arrived in Johannesburg at the same time, and this helped. The Witwatersrand was the biggest gold-field ever discovered, and fortunes were being made. Abe was able in a comparatively short time to turn the £4000 he had borrowed into £30,000 in the bank, and it was at this point that he decided to give up stockbroking and turn to speculating in property for himself.

One of his first buys was the Pilgrim's Rest goldmine – the one whose potential had first lured him to the Transvaal gold-fields. Later he bought the Kleinfontein mine – influenced by its name, which was that of his childhood home where his mother had died. Abe had a sentimental, almost superstitious streak. But sentiment was aligned with immense toughness. He was in the toughest environment in the world. He had a flair for making deals; a shrewd ability to assess the value of mining and building land unrecognized by others. He soon gained control of the Transvaal

Goldmining estates, but, not wanting to run them himself, transferred their management to the Wernher/Beit partnership, while remaining a director. Later he became a major shareholder in Rand Mines, along with some of the great names in gold-mining: Julius Wernher, Alfred Beit, Hermann Eckstein, Lionel Phillips and the Rothschilds, all of whom had started their fortune-building in the diamond mining in Kimberley.

All through this meteoric rise in his fortunes, Abe maintained his interest in sport. He was rich enough now to own racehorses, and consistently made money on the racecourse, once winning £64,000 by backing his own horse in the Johannesburg Handicap. His greatest love at that time was cricket, learned at his English schools. By 1891 he was captain of the Wanderers Cricket Club in Johannesburg. He also played polo, and he launched the South African Amateur Athletic Association, of which he became president.

By 1894 he had £100,000 in the bank, and was chairman of the Johannesburg Stock Exchange. He was a town councillor. He was described in the *Golden Transvaal* (a London publication) as 'the most daring speculator of the Golden City'. He was twenty-nine.

Abe now felt secure enough to get married. Caroline Paddon was the daughter of a wealthy Kimberley merchant who also owned a large house in south London, and this was where their wedding took place in 1894. He brought Caroline back to Johannesburg and installed her in Clewer House, his fine new house in the suburb of Belgravia.

A few years earlier, two men had entered Abe's life whose influence was soon to change the direction of his ambitions. Cecil John Rhodes, as the controller of 90 per cent of the world's diamond production (after the amalgamation of the Central Company and De Beers in 1888), had turned his attention to gold-mining, but at first his interest was not wholehearted; his attention was on other matters. He and Leander Starr Jameson were involved in establishing a Protectorate over Chief Lobengula's Matabele kingdom in Western Zambesia. In 1888 Rhodes was granted a 'concession' which gave him a monopoly over the exploitation of mineral rights in the whole of Zambesia and Mashonaland. He formed the British

South Africa Company, which became known as the Chartered Company, having been granted its charter by Queen Victoria. Shortly after it was formed, Rhodes asked Abe to join the Chartered Company, and allowed him a share in all its ventures. This culminated, many years later, in Abe becoming the biggest landowner in Rhodesia.

'Bailey is a man after my own heart,' Rhodes declared. 'He does things and wastes neither my time nor his own.' Abe was not, however, one of Rhodes's chosen young acolytes, of whom there were many. He was a man whom Rhodes recognized as an astute business partner: a man on whom he could rely totally, but not, as his praise implies, an intimate. The effect of Rhodes's personality on Abe, however, was electrifying.

'Rhodes warmed me up, raised me from the ground and lighted up my path.' It was Rhodes's imperialism, and his vision of South Africa as a country with all its various colonies and protectorates united, forming a union that would be a vital part of the British Empire, that inspired and delighted Abe. He believed this to be the way in which his beloved South Africa could be brought to its fullest potential, and become a country of influence in the world. He saw in Rhodes the man who could achieve this, and was inspired by him to become a political activist.

One stumbling block in the path of these empire builders was the portly figure of the Boer president of the Transvaal, or the South African Republic: Stephanus Johannes Paulus Kruger. In 1895 he was seventy, and had been president of the Transvaal for twelve years. Although enthusiastic about the huge finds of gold on his territory, he disliked and mistrusted the influx of foreigners – *uitlanders* – that had been tempted into the Transvaal, and had amassed for themselves such huge fortunes. He reaped bountiful taxes from them, but, although they outnumbered the Boers in the Transvaal, Kruger refused to allow them a vote in the government elections. They resented this inordinately.

Rhodes and Jameson and their cronies had long opposed Kruger's policies, but to no avail. He was intransigent. The result of their frustration was the notorious Jameson Raid of 1895, which was to be the trigger for the second, savage, Boer War. Winston

Churchill later said of the Jameson Raid that it was the 'event which seems to me when I look back over the map of my life to be the fountain of all ill'. Abe did not agree.

He had joined the Reform Committee when it was formed in 1895, in order to back any action to oust Kruger from his leadership. The Corner House, a powerful group of 'Randlords', which included Beit, Wernher, Phillips, Eckstein and Percy Fitzpatrick, was the main force behind the Reform Committee. Cecil Rhodes's brother Frank, who ran the huge consortium of gold-mines called Goldfields, was also involved. Inspired by the involvement of Rhodes in the movement, if only through his brother, Abe threw himself into the enterprise of planning the Jameson Raid.

The Reform Committee was meant to provide support and resources within Johannesburg when the projected raid on the town took place. Arms were to be taken to the Wanderers Cricket Club when the time for the raid had been decided. Jameson had promised not to start the raid until he had heard from the Reformers that they were ready to support him. But he broke his promise, and launched the raid without telling them, with disastrous consequences.

Abe had helped to finance the raid, but was not in Johannesburg when it happened; he was returning home from England. As far as he knew, negotiations were still going on between the *uitlanders* and Kruger. When he arrived home 30 December he was handed a cryptic telegram: 'The veterinary surgeon says the horses are now all right. He started last night will reach you on Wednesday. He says he can back himself for £700. Signed Godolphin.' The raid had started the day before. Godolphin was the code name for Dr Rutherford Harris, a confidant of Jameson. Abe immediately showed the telegram to the rest of the Reformers, and then became involved in a desperate effort to collect and distribute arms, and rush them to the Wanderers Cricket Club, but it was a lost cause. Within four days Jameson's raiders had surrendered and been rounded up by Boer forces.

The Pretoria government had a list of all the members of the Reform Committee, and they were immediately arrested and put in jail. Abe, along with sixty-five other collaborators, was given a three-year sentence. Here his father proved useful to him. Thomas Bailey, as an Afrikanerbond member of the Cape parliament, was considered pro-Boer. He interceded with President Kruger on behalf of his son. Kruger reportedly responded: 'You have not brought your son up properly. I am going to teach him a lesson.' But Abe's prison sentence, and that of his co-prisoners, was reduced to a fine of £2000, which was paid for all the prisoners by subscriptions from the Chamber of Mines, the Mining Magnates, and the Johannesburg Stock Exchange.

While he was on trial, a cricket team he had invited over from England, led by Lord Hawke, arrived in Cape Town. Abe had hoped to meet them when they arrived, but had to send Lord Hawke a telegram saying he was 'unavoidably elsewhere', which caused much laughter among the cricketers.

During the following three years he brought out Lord Hawke's team again, amongst whom was the legendary W.G. Grace. Abe had the effrontery to bowl him the newly invented 'googly', which bemused the great man. 'Which way do you come, which way do you come?' Grace shouted at Abe, walking down the pitch at the end of the over. History doesn't relate whether Abe bowled him out.

In 1899 the Boer War began. Abe had been in England for much of that year, but when war broke out he immediately returned to South Africa. He had no experience of fighting, but his knowledge of Afrikaans was invaluable, and he knew the country extremely well. He was made an Intelligence Officer, serving with General Pole-Carew's 9th Brigade. He was taken prisoner by the Boers after the battle of Elandsfontein, on 9 May 1900, but managed to escape – in time to take part in the battle of Diamond Hill thirteen days later.

After Johannesburg and Pretoria were occupied by the British, the Boers turned to guerrilla warfare. Abe was able to equip British forces operating against them with horses and vehicles, which he paid for himself. He joined in chasing the guerrillas, among whom was Jan Smuts, one of their bravest and most elusive commanders.

At the end of the war Abe had been mentioned in despatches twice, and decorated with the King's and Queen's medals with five clasps. He had also met Winston Churchill, another prisoner of war who escaped. They were to remain close friends for the rest of Abe's life. Abe brought about the meeting of Winston Churchill and Cecil Rhodes, shortly before Rhodes's death in 1902. In August 1901 Rhodes had taken a shooting lodge in Scotland. Abe brought his young protégé Churchill with him. (Churchill was ten years younger than Abe.) Churchill remembered it thus: 'We rode ponies and carried guns and engaged in various affairs, nominally sporting.' Rhodes's comment on Churchill was, 'He is a young man who will go far if he doesn't overbalance.'

The war ended in June 1902. Rhodes had died in March 1902. By then Abe had two children. His devotion and admiration for Rhodes was such that he had named his children Cecil (a daughter, born in 1896) and John (born in 1900). Another devastating loss for Abe in 1902 was the death of his young wife Caroline, leaving him the lone parent of a six-year-old daughter and a two-year-old son. He himself was very ill that year. It was a traumatic time for him, but, with characteristic resilience, he set about rebuilding his life.

The years 1902–11 – between the death of his first wife and his marriage to Mary Westenra – were years of extraordinary activity for Abe. He put his mines back into production, and rebuilt his racing stables. He stood for Rhodes's seat in the Cape parliament, which he won, and remained M.P. there for three years. When Jameson became Prime Minister of the Cape in 1904, Abe became his Chief Whip, and their friendship was cemented. During this time he also took on Sir Herbert Baker's designs for the new house he had been building for Rhodes, in Muizenberg, called 'Rust-en-Vrede' – Rest and Peace in Afrikaans. When Rhodes died all that had been completed were the perimeter walls and the foundations. Abe and Herbert Baker completed the house, with double-storied Dutch gables on two façades, in a fine position under an over-hanging terraced garden looking out across Muizenberg Bay, in 1905. It still exists much as it was in Abe's day, with similar Cape Dutch furniture. It is not enormous, but it was large enough for Abe to entertain lavishly. He liked to have about sixteen people to dinner nearly every night, and his gift was to bring people of influence from different walks of life together, encouraging them to help to make things happen.

He became the owner of Rhodes's 1.25-million-acre ranch in Rhodesia, called Rhodesdale, thereby becoming the largest individual owner of land in Rhodesia. Later Rhodesdale was merged into the firm Abe founded, London and Rhodesian Mining and Land Co., known as Lonrho. He also farmed three hundred square miles of the Karoo, on which Herbert Baker built him a single-storied thatched house. The farm was called Clewer. He bred merino sheep there, as well as breeding his racehorses.

In 1908 Abe decided he was needed in the Transvaal parliament, where the Prime Minister was General Botha. Abe's desire was for the British and the Boer factions of South Africa to be able to co-operate, and carry out Rhodes's plan for a Union of South Africa within the British Empire. He was made Whip in the Pretoria government. His relationship with Botha was good. At the end of the Boer War, although they had been opponents, Abe had lent Botha money to buy a house. Botha once described Abe as 'the most spectacular character in South Africa'. It is easy to understand why he thought this. Abe's range of interests, his wealth, his energy, dedication to good causes, generosity, foresightedness, panache, flair – all were indeed spectacular. He became a newspaper magnate, establishing the magazine *African World* in London, and buying the *Rand Daily Mail* and the *Sunday Times*, two important Johannesburg papers. He did all he could to encourage British settlers to come to the Dutch Transvaal, initiating schemes for young men to be given tracts of land to farm, with grants supplied by himself. He was instrumental in forming the Closer Union Society, backing it financially and through Union Clubs which he had started through the country. The Union Club in Johannesburg in particular was a powerhouse of Unionist politics. At this point Botha is said to have thought of Abe as his successor, though that never came to pass. Abe also started *The State* magazine, which propagated the gospel of a Union of South Africa, and later, when it had done its job, he helped to finance a quarterly magazine, *The Round Table*.

The Union of South Africa was born in 1910, eight years after Rhodes's death, and three weeks after the death of King Edward VII of England. In March 1911 Abe was created K.C.M.G. –

Knight Commander of St Michael and St George. This was an honour only in the gift of the King, and the new monarch, George V, presented it to him in recognition of all the work he had done to bring about the Union of South Africa. He was one of the invited guests in Westminster Abbey to witness the coronation. In this year he met Mary, and joined the Rossmore family as Derry's son-in-law. Did they realize what a phenomenal man had joined their family? And did Abe realize what he had undertaken, in marrying Mary?

6

An Unlikely Pair

When Mittie Naylor married Derry Rossmore in 1882, her father gave her a dowry of £1000 a year. For a man who was known as the richest commoner in England this was not a gigantic amount, but it was the equivalent of perhaps £60,000 a year today. Derry, when he 'gave' his daughter in marriage to Sir Abe Bailey, must have been aware that the boot was entirely on the other foot. In September 1911, the month of Mary's wedding, a considerable sum of money, in debentures, shares and cash, was paid by Abe into a trust held in the names of Mary herself, her father, and two other trustees – Arthur Ward (solicitor) and Oscar Schwartz (stock-broker). The money was distributed as follows:

> £30,000 debentures in South African Gold Mines Ltd.
> 20,000 shares of £1 each in the Pretoria Townships Ltd.
> £20,000 debentures in East Rand Property Mines Ltd.
> $25,000 Chesapeake and Ohio Railway $4^1/2\%$ Convertible Gold Bonds 1930.
> $30,000 Cincinnati Hamilton and Dayton Railway Co. First and refunding Mortgage 4% Gold Bonds 1959 (guaranteed by Baltimore and Ohio Railroad Co.).
> £9,400 Southern San Paulo Railway 5% debentures.
> $25,000 Erie Railroad Prior Lien 4% Bonds 1996.
> £6,000 St Paul and Kansas City Short Line Railroad Co. First Mortgage $4^1/2\%$ Gold Bonds 1941.
> £2,000 cash.

Because this trust was made over to both Mary and her father, it could not be seen exactly as down payment for Mary's hand – she was to benefit from it, presumably, as well as her father. But there can be little doubt that had that payment not been available and forthcoming, the marriage would not have taken place.

For they were an unlikely pair. There was a gap of twenty-six years between them. Mary was a very young twenty-year-old. Her life had up till then been the sheltered life of a child – she had only been 'out' in the world for a mere two years, and those had been spent in the company of her parents' friends and their children, all of her own background. She was just beginning to make forays of her own across the Irish Sea to stay with her Aunt Doods for the hunting in Leicestershire and Northamptonshire, but otherwise her life was circumscribed. This didn't mean that it wasn't enjoyable – it was everything she loved best, and she had begun to make a reputation for herself as a sportswoman and something of a whirlwind, cheerfully dashing from one sporting fixture to the next.

Sir Abe Bailey, born in 1864, was only three years younger than Mittie, and eleven years younger than Derry. He was easily old enough to be Mary's father. As well as this difference, he was an immensely experienced man of the world, having been out earning his own money from an early age, and having lived most of his life in the demanding environment of turn-of-the-century South Africa. He had been married for seven years, until the death of his wife in 1902, and he had two young children. He had spent some days in prison. Inevitably, from so much buffeting by forces and circumstances, he had by the age of forty-six become a tough negotiator, confident in the position he had carved for himself in the world. He was a man of power, and above all a great businessman. To a young innocent like Mary, Abe must have seemed something of a Colossus, and she must have been amazed and flattered that he wanted to marry her.

There is no evidence of where they first met. Abe and Derry were definitely both invited guests in Westminster Abbey at the Coronation of King George V in June 1911, three months before Abe and Mary's wedding. If they first met there, or during celebrations surrounding the event, it would have been a remarkably speedy arrangement for them to be secretly engaged two months later, but not impossible, given a lot of determination on both sides.

The meeting might have come about through Derry's and Abe's mutual interest in horse-racing. By 1911 Derry had been forbidden by his irate father-in-law to own any more race horses himself, but he was not forbidden the race course, and it is likely that his and Abe's paths would have crossed, at Epsom or Ascot or Newmarket. It is not difficult to imagine Derry and Mittie being impressed by Abe's accomplishments, character and wealth.

The engagement was announced in the papers in mid-August. In London this was an unusual time of the year for a society wedding, as the Season was over. People had left London and disappeared to their grouse moors and their fishing rivers. Mittie had to put up with this. The big fish had been caught: he must be landed, whatever the difficulties. Too much playing of the line could easily lose him.

Abe's paper *The African World* of 9 September 1911, after commenting on the unfashionable time for the wedding, went on: 'The beauty, youth and personal charm of the bride; her great social success, when, as one of the loveliest debutantes, she made her first appearance two seasons ago; her reputed skill and daring in the hunting field, all contributed to the public curiosity and interest. As a consequence, an immense crowd gathered outside Holy Trinity Church Sloane Street.'

Holy Trinity Sloane Street is no longer the fashionable church it was then. It is just north of Sloane Square, the west door leading out directly on to the Sloane Street pavement. It is an interesting church, modern in Mary's day, having been consecrated in the year she was born, 1890. It was designed by John Dando Sedding, a leading member of the Arts and Crafts movement. The cost of the church was borne by Earl Cadogan, on whose estate it was built. He became Lord Lieutenant of Ireland shortly after the church was consecrated, and Derry and Mittie knew him well when he lived in the Viceregal Lodge in Phoenix Park, Dublin. The most immediate reason for their choosing that church was that at the time of the wedding Derry and Mittie were renting a flat in Wellesley House, Lower Sloane Street, and it was necessary for Mary to be married, and to have her banns read, in a church in the same parish. The banns had to be read for three Sundays before the wedding: they were just able to fit this in before 5 September.

At the time of the wedding the organ in the church was being repaired. Abe Bailey therefore arranged, in his typically munificent fashion, to provide an adequate organ for the service, and a special choir was also brought in.

For the wedding the church was decorated with immense palms on either side of the chancel steps, and masses of sweet-smelling lilies, spirea and asters. More than four hundred people were there. Mary's dress, though described in the *Northern Standard* as 'a triumph of chic simplicity', sounds as though it was most complicated. It was of

> gold and white brocade, in semi-princesse form, draped with exquisite pointe-de-Venise lace. The train was not very long and somewhat narrow, and down one side of it was a straight embroidered panel. The bodice had a kimono of ivory chiffon, cut low at the front, with chiffon sleeves finished at the elbows. Over the shoulders was draped some antique Venetian dentelle, so arranged that it formed stoles. The ends were then caught at the waist with a cluster of orange blossoms and tulle veil.

Mary had six bridesmaids – cousins, friends, and Abe's daughter Cecil, who was sixteen, the same age as Mary's younger brother Richard. The bridesmaids were dressed in a mixture of flesh-pink charmeuse and pale blue. Over their shoulders they wore scarves of pale blue chiffon edged with lace, and long white gloves. Instead of hats, folds of blue chiffon were arranged round their hair, fastened with multi-coloured silk flowers and leaves. Each wore on the corsage a brooch in the shape of a lover's knot, made of rubies and diamonds, the gift of the bridegroom. As bouquets they had bunches of pink carnations tied with blue satin ribbon. It was a very pretty, feminine wedding.

The crowd of onlookers, milling about in Sloane Street among the horse-drawn buses, were not only there to gape at the bride and bridesmaids – there was another riveting focus of attention. Abe Bailey had asked his old crony and one-time fellow prisoner, Sir Leander Starr Jameson, to be his best man. In 1911 he was still famous in England, and the crowd was agog to see him. But they were disappointed. He and Abe slid discreetly into the church through the vestry door. The crowd's only glimpse of him would have been as he left the church at the end of the service with the rest of the congregation, among whom were plenty of other interesting faces for the crowd to gawp at.

The Duchess of Newcastle, Mary's first cousin, was there. Derry's older sister Frances had married a Major Henry 'Sugar' Candy, and their daughter married the Duke of Newcastle. She was known to the family as Tatta. From Ireland came the Earl and Countess of Kilmoray (he was one of the signatories on the marriage certificate; the Earl of Iveagh was another). Lady Constance Leslie was there, from Glaslough in Co. Monaghan. The Marchioness of Linlithgow appeared at the wedding reception, as did Mrs George Cornwallis West, who was Winston Churchill's mother. Although a very good friend of Abe's, Winston himself was not at the wedding – he was in Scotland – but he did send a present.

The reception was held in 39 Portman Square, which was the home of Lord Tredegar, a good friend of Derry's. Mittie had held a special reception the day before the wedding so that the presents could be admired; she ordered special glass cabinets to house the most valuable objects. Abe gave his bride a high diamond tiara. There is a picture of Mary wearing it when she was presented at court for the second time, as a married woman. He also gave her a necklace: a long chain of diamonds finished with two pear-shaped pearls, and a diamond corsage ornament set with two enormous sapphires surrounded with diamonds. Jameson gave her a feather-shaped diamond brooch, which could be worn as either a corsage or a hair ornament. Her parents gave her a diamond necklace, and her brothers William and Richard gave her a diamond brooch in the shape of a spider.

In the photograph of Mary as a bride on the arm of her bridegroom, there is a faraway, bemused look in her eyes. Abe, beside her, looks determined but detached. Wedding photographs in those days were meant to be very formal, and were not conducive to natural expressions. But even so, radiant happiness was sometimes able to break through. Not in this case.

According to Mary's children, Mary was only told by Mittie the night before her wedding what were known as 'the facts of life'. To be married to someone whom you hardly know, who is not of your own choosing, of your own age, or even of your own country, is daunting enough. But to be told what is to be expected of this union the very next day, and to be told that such behaviour was right, proper and her duty, must have been quite a severe shock. Some of her children say that she never quite recovered from that shock, and as a result was excessively prudish all her life. When her son Jim said he wanted to breed from one of his ponies, she expressed horror at such an idea. She would not allow any conversation about stallions covering mares. She attempted to seal up a door between two adjoining rooms when her brother and his intended bride were sleeping in them. And she was most discouraging when her children showed signs of wanting to become more closely involved with people of the opposite sex. In spite of all this, however, she and Abe did manage to produce five children together.

After the reception, Mary and Abe left London and went down to Abe's house Yewhurst, near East Grinstead in Sussex. They stayed there for the next two days. It is likely that Abe's children, John and Cecil, went with them. They sailed to Ireland, for Abe's first visit to that country, three days later, on Friday 8 September. They travelled overnight by boat to Belfast, and on down to Monaghan early the next morning by train, arriving at the station at 9.50 a.m.

Monaghan had been preparing for them with great enthusiasm. Mary was most popular in her home town. The Rossmores were the nearest thing the inhabitants had to royalty, and Mary had endeared herself to them by her sportsmanship and courage, as well as by her good looks and cheerfulness. So the town had decided to make a great day of her homecoming with her wealthy husband.

As they stepped onto the platform they were greeted by a crowd of people, among whom were Mary's father and her two brothers. Mary was given a bouquet of pink roses by the little son of the

Chairman of the Urban District Council. When they came out of the station, they were met by cheering crowds lining their route, and specially erected poles carrying swirling banners of green and gold bunting, all through the town. More flowers were given to Mary, and then the family climbed into two splendid motor cars which were waiting outside the station. The cars drove through all the principal streets of the town, through crowds who lined their route and cheered lustily as they passed. The drive to Rossmore Park was not very far, and when they arrived at the gates they saw that these had been specially decorated, with a massive banner inscribed 'Cead Míle Fáilte' – a hundred thousand welcomes. As they wound up the long drive they came to another banner – 'May Happiness Attend You', in English. And when they drove up to the castle itself they found a huge banner, festooned with roses, which read simply 'HOME'.

The family disappeared inside the castle and were not seen again until 4 p.m., when they were summoned out to the front steps to find the Monaghan Brass Band and the Flute Band of the Irish National Foresters blowing their hearts out, as well as a delegation from the Monaghan Urban Council who had arrived to make a formal presentation to Mary and Abe. The gift, paid for by sub-scription, was a splendid Georgian silver epergne, with its massive branches holding Waterford glass confit dishes. Mary's brother William had his box camera, and took a photograph of Mary and Abe standing in the front door of the house, along with the com-mittee in their top hats and the vast epergne standing grandly on a table in between. Abe is leaning at his ease against the jamb of the open door; Mary is wearing a most becoming cream linen suit, with a long skirt to the ground, and a pink hat lined with black with a pink plume. She looked delightful – and she looked happy. William took another photograph of her a few minutes later, standing on the gravel with an old friend of the family, Mr Smith, and she is laugh-ing and looking relaxed: she is home, back in her beloved Monaghan again.

Speeches were made: Mr Francis Tierney, the Chairman of the Monaghan District Council, went first, and his speech was touch-ingly affectionate.

Lady Bailey, it is my privilege to have the honour on this auspicious occasion of making you the presentation so quickly organised by some of your friends. The presentation is from a few friends only, for as you know everyone around Monaghan, young and old, rich and poor, should like to have been on the list of subscribers, for everyone who knows you loves you, and while we are glad in your joy, yet we feel the parting is near. Your lot is to be cast in another country, and we hope and pray that you may have every joy and happiness there, but we venture to say you will have no dearer friends and no warmer-hearted good wishes than those around your own native place, for your family, and especially yourself, have completely won the affection of the people.

Several other dignitaries of Monaghan then had their say. The central point of the next speech, by a Mr Denis Carolan Rushe, B.A., was that 'he was delighted to see the unanimity of the people of Monaghan assembled there that day. Bands of every political view were represented and people of every political persuasion were assembled to do honour to the daughter of Lord and Lady Rossmore.'

There were a few other speeches, and then Abe made a reply, on behalf of himself and Mary. He was speaking off the cuff, as he always did.

Ladies and Gentlemen – I might say friends of my wife, you good people of Monaghan. I have noticed the congratulations accorded to my wife upon marrying myself. I think these congratulations are upon trust. You know nothing of me – at any rate, very little, and it is for me to prove a good husband to my wife. (Applause.) But when it comes to congratulating her it is quite a different point: she has lived amongst you for many years, and from what I know of her own feelings with regard to these parts, you have every right to think well of her. She loves her home, she loves her country, and she loves her people, and when a person does that, he or she deserves well of her people.

He went on to talk of the political divisions between the two races in Ireland, comparing them to the division between the two races in his own country – by which he meant English and Dutch, ignoring the Africans – and he said how glad he was to know of Lord Rossmore's reputation as a peacemaker.

The next presentation was specifically to Mary – a gold hunting horn, from the Monaghan Harriers, presented by Captain Irwin, who was the Master of Hounds before Mary, and had become secretary to the hunt. Mary made a brief reply of thanks, and the ceremony was over. Later that night there was a display of fireworks over the castle.

Mary had been blessed with perfect weather for her return to her home, just as she had been blessed by brilliant sunshine on the day of her wedding in London. All was set fair for her, it seemed. Three days later she and Abe travelled back to England, and a week later, on 23 September, they set sail for South Africa.

7

Married Life, 1911–1926

The R.M.S. *Saxon*, which carried Abe and Mary down to the Cape after their wedding, was a ship of the Union Castle Line. In 1857 the line had successfully tendered for the mail service between England and South Africa, and this was its only route. The *Saxon* was a luxurious passenger liner of 10,000 tons, built by Harland and Wolff in Belfast, with inlaid mahogany furniture upholstered in figured morocco leather, and teak and satinwood panelling under a vast dome of stained glass in the first-class lounge.

Mary and Abe travelled first class. The journey – almost six thousand miles – took three to four weeks, usually stopping in Madeira en route.

On a sea voyage of three weeks or more the horizons of everyday life narrow very quickly to the immediate confines of the ship itself; past and future are suspended, and the activities organized by the ship's purser – concerts, deck tennis, dancing in the evening, a fancy-dress ball – seem of paramount importance. Abe and Mary took part in it all. They might have seemed to the other passengers to be more like father and daughter than husband and wife, but Abe was still a comparatively young and virile man at forty-six; he was also a sportsman, and played deck cricket merrily with the rest. And Mary, still somewhat dazed by her swift transformation from post-debutante to tycoon's wife, must have loved the good-humoured fun of the shipboard entertainments. But she had learned, during the two years since her coming out, how to behave with sophistication and poise. In those two years she had been a guest in some of the richest and most splendid country houses in England and Ireland, and even in Austria. From her photograph albums a list can be made: there are pictures of Mary between 1908 and 1911 at Elveden, the home of the Earl of Iveagh; Tidworth House, Andover, the home of Lord Basil Blackwood; Badminton House in Wiltshire, the Duke of Beaufort's seat; Mourne Park, Newry, of the Earl of Needham; Duntreath Castle, Blanefield (where she drew a maliciously funny caricature of Violet Keppel); Shipley Hall, Derby; Castle Frankenstein in Austria – and many more.

Then, she had her mother to advise her as to which gloves and what hat to wear, how to comport herself at the dinner table, and to whom she should be especially polite. Now, she had her new husband Abe. Her only other ally was her maid, but we know from her letter to her brother that she was newly employed, and probably as much at sea in every sense as Mary.

It is probable that they travelled with a suite of rooms, including two staterooms, as was the custom at that time, and their own sitting room. What could they have had to talk about, after the first few days of reminiscing about the wedding and the jaunt to Ireland? For the first time Mary had none of her dogs with her, and certainly none of her horses, and no brothers to fool about with; she was mercifully free from her mother's restraining eagle eye, but she was also without her beloved father. She had, by degrees, to find clues to the most interesting but strange man she had married – a being from a different universe, with a life behind him of experiences totally unknown to her, whose mind was perpetually filled, even on board ship, with the complexities and machinations of his vast world of business. Perhaps, like Desdemona and Othello, as he told her his tales of astonishing feats and fearful disasters, she grew to admire and then to find more and more affection for him. Certainly in those early weeks she could not have realized what later became so apparent – that their characters, both formed of granite, would, through the years, crash against each other with resounding force.

The ship docked in Cape Town in the middle of October. Abe

took Mary straight to his house, which looked over Muizenberg Bay, about twenty miles outside of Cape Town. After Rossmore Castle, Rust-en-Vrede would seem a modest house to Mary, but a spectacularly attractive one, set only fifty yards from the sea, with a steep cliff of terraced gardens rising up behind it, and its characteristic Cape Dutch gables. It is not a mansion – more a villa – and Mary can have had few qualms as to how she would be able to run it, for Abe had a small army of servants who already knew his needs and his likes and dislikes. They arrived there in South Africa's spring, an ideal time for Abe to show Mary his beloved country, and very soon they set out on their travels.

There were so many things to show her. He had his house, Friedenburg, in Johannesburg; he had his farms in Colesberg in the Karoo; and, more impressive than all these, the million and a half acres that he owned in Rhodesia. On 27 October they were at the Victoria Falls, and a few days later at Rhodes's grave, up among the strange round boulders in the Matopo hills, in the place known as the World's View. By now Mary knew of her husband's hero-worship of Rhodes; she knew too that he had stood for and won Rhodes's seat in the Cape parliament, that the house in Muizenberg had originally been planned for Rhodes by the great architect Sir Herbert Baker, and that the vast tracts of land in Rhodesia now belonging to Abe were once the property of Rhodes. It was an emotional moment for Abe, nine years after Rhodes's death, to show his tomb to Mary. When Abe died, twenty-nine years later, his choice of burial place reflected his need to be buried as Rhodes had been: high on a hillside, above Rust-en-Vrede, with a panoramic view of sea and distant mountaintops.

These two months of travelling were their honeymoon. But Mary and Abe were not to be left to their own devices any longer. On 25 November Mary's father and two brothers set sail from Southampton to visit them. The main reason given was the health of Mary's younger brother Dick, which was causing anxiety, but it may be that Derry wanted to see with his own eyes what he had let his daughter in for: was she going to be happy with the man who had so obligingly stepped in to their lives and saved Derry's own bacon?

Abe and Mary had got back to Johannesburg from Rhodesia on 2 December, in time for her to perform her first ceremony as the wife of a politician (although Abe did not like to think of himself as a politician). She was invited to open a bazaar in aid of a local Roman Catholic church, in what had been and was to be again his constituency of Krugersdorp. Mary made a short speech, and was then presented with a fan made of ostrich feathers set in gold and decorated with diamonds and emeralds. Abe made a speech as well. He told the people of Krugersdorp that if they wanted to remain prosperous, they should not put their faith in the mines; they should encourage their children to work instead on the land. He himself was a farmer as well as everything else, and he loved to see the land being properly cultivated.

A few days after this, Mary's father and brothers arrived. Abe's children were probably there too, and he had, for the first time in many years, a most cheerful Christmas – Mary's first summer Christmas. While they were all there in Rust-en-Vrede Mary and her brothers showed their intrepid characters by deciding to swim across the bay, from Muizenberg to Kalk Bay: a distance of about three miles. Mary was bursting with energy, and loved having her brothers to compete with in outdoor feats. Kalk Bay was where Abe kept his yacht, inevitably called *Clewer*. Mary would often swim huge distances out to sea. Her son Jim remembers that on one occasion a man, seeing her disappearing over the horizon, rowed out to rescue her, and when he arrived she cursed him roundly for interfering.

They all stayed until March, when Mary and Abe went back on the same boat with them to England. Just before Derry had left for South Africa he and Mittie had been given, by the newly crowned King George and Queen Mary, a Grace and Favour residence at Hampton Court, called The Stud House. 'Grace and Favour' meant that the house still belonged to the Crown, but they could live in it free of rent for the rest of their lives. This privilege was usually granted to people who had given distinguished service to the state, such as retired field marshals or admirals. Derry did not fall into this category. Although some of Mary's descendants think this honour was due to Mittie's sexual friendship with King George

V's father, Edward VII, it is much more likely to have been a result of Mittie's close friendship with Queen Mary, which lasted all their lives, and long after they both became widows. Mittie's grandchildren remember her expressing what was almost exasperation when Queen Mary sent word that she wanted to come and visit her – it obviously happened so often. The new house near London was a godsend to Mittie, who loved to escape in the summer from Monaghan and be part of all the social festivities of the London season. And renting a London flat, as they had previously done, was a fearful drain on Derry's emptying pocket. But Mittie hurried back to Rossmore in February, in order to be ready for Mary and Abe's return there in March: she knew that that was, of all places, the one where Mary would most long to be.

The ships of the Union Castle Line were to become drearily familiar places to Mary during the next thirty years of her life. Abe had set the pattern already, of continual dashes from one hemisphere to the other. They seldom seemed to spend more than a few months in South Africa before they steamed north again. Abe had his large house in Sussex, and Mary had her parents' houses in Hampton Court and Monaghan. All too quickly she realized which hemisphere she liked better. South African society did not appeal to her. She found it provincial. She missed her hunting. Above all, she missed County Monaghan and the Irish bogs, and the humour and whimsy of the Irish. She did not return to South Africa until September 1912, after five happy months in England and Ireland.

During this time Derry became famous and notorious, upon the publication of *Things I Can Tell*. Anita Leslie, Sir Shane's daughter, wrote in her book *Edwardians in Love* that Derry Rossmore 'is the sole Edwardian who actually relates stories in print concerning his own escapades, which in the parlance of the time were "roguey-poguey"'. So roguey-poguey they were that the book became a best seller, and Derry gained a dubious reputation at the age of fifty-nine: that of a rake with questionable morals and taste. The book went into a second edition, and presumably earned him some much-needed money – and lost him some too, with law cases for libel.

We can only guess at Mary's reaction to her father's book. She loved him dearly and had probably had to forgive him for plenty of peccadilloes already. She was his ally when trouble brewed up between him and Mittie, and most likely her laugh, which everyone remembers as having the same booming decibels as her father's, roared out in defensive sympathy. Mary's time in England and Ireland must have been plagued by the many and varied reactions to this outrageous and somewhat absurd book.

While Mary and Abe were in London in 1912 they stayed at the Ritz Hotel. One event in August must have thrilled Mary: F.K. McClean flew his aeroplane under Tower Bridge on the Thames. By then aeroplanes were becoming more familiar objects in the sky. Geoffrey de Havilland, who had built his first aeroplane in 1909, was developing an important new range of them. He was later to play a most vital part in Mary's life, when she first learned to fly at his aerodrome in 1926.

In December 1912 Mary and Abe were back in England, at a pheasant shoot at Cadland, near Southampton. A group photograph of the guns and their wives shows Mary smiling happily, perched on a shooting stick. She is the only wife not standing. Abe looks his usual benign, sturdy self. He was a superb shot, and made sure that he was in England or Scotland for the shooting season. Through the years he rented a variety of large houses and shoots in different parts of the country, and lavishly entertained his influential friends. In this he was again following the example of Rhodes, who himself took houses in Scotland in order to entertain the mighty and great on the grouse moors.

Mary and Abe's first child, a daughter born in August 1913, was christened Mittie Mary Starr – Mittie, after her grandmother; Mary, after her mother and perhaps her illustrious ancestor Mary Lady Blayney; and Starr, after Abe's great political ally Leander Starr Jameson, who was no doubt asked to be the baby's godfather. She was known as Mary Ellen as a child, and later simply Mary, or M.E. She remained Mary's only child until 1918, when twins were born, so for five years she reigned supreme in the nursery. But it was not a conventionally safe and cosy childhood. Mary and Abe decided that their children should be brought up in England. Whenever Mary went back to South Africa her children were left behind.

In May 1913, in order to have a permanent home in London for

Mary and the forthcoming child, and to entertain as he did in Rust-en-Vrede, Abe rented 38 Bryanston Square. The square is in central London just north of Mayfair and Oxford Street, and number 38 was an impressive five-storey house. It had a wide entrance hall, a dining-room large enough to seat thirty people with ease, a fine drawing-room and two lifts – one for people and one for luggage. In front of the house was the private garden of the square, and behind was the cobbled mews. This was to be the home in which Mary's children were brought up. The high third floor was their domain, up until 1930, when Abe found a house in Oxfordshire where they could live more happily in the country.

Abe scribbled a quick note to Mary in 1913, when they were moving into 38 Bryanston Square:

> Take what beds you really want for 38 B.S. from Yewhurst if you cannot do better at Heals for beds. I would like a larger bed. I don't care for a single bed. You must organise your show better than you do. It is not necessary for you to do so much. Give Nugent[?] her instructions and let her do it.
>
> Do you want any of the furniture or tapestries from Rust-en-Vrede or shall I sell it if it is possible with the house, as I cannot keep so many establishments going? Please cable me to A.B. Muizenberg – if we keep the little cottage and Colesberg estate they should be enough for the present. Leave all the modern furniture at Yewhurst. If you wish for any of the things from Mrs. James [the landlady] she may wish to sell some of the furniture – don't buy anything *without consulting* me *please*. Get Leggats to order your picture to be engraved …

Abe gained a reputation for lavish entertaining at 38 Bryanston Square between the wars. His chef had been brought from Buckingham Palace. Abe's son Jim writes: 'Peers, statesmen, financiers, sportsmen and intellectuals smacked their lips at the prospect of an invitation to dine at Bryanston Square.' Sir Robert Boothby, a politician, described dinner there in the thirties:

Dined with Sir Abe Bailey. A most swagger affair, all men.

Above: *Rossmore Castle*
Left: *Mittie*
Below: *Derry with his children Richard, Mary, and William (kneeling)*

1

Mary aged nineteen, with her dogs

2

Above left: *William, Richard and Mary*
Above right: *Mary at the time of her presentation
   at court, 1909*
Right: *Caricature of Derry by Mary*

A shooting party at Elveden, Suffolk, home of Lord Iveagh, 1908. Mary is standing, second from right; the future king George V is standing second from left

Photo from the family album, taken in Co. Londonderry c. 1902, in which Mittie's face has been scratched out

4

Abe Bailey, photographed in Queenstown, Cape Colony; and (right) a cartoon of Abe from The African World *in 1909 encouraging whites in South Africa to farm the land*

Abe and Mary at Rossmore after their wedding in 1911, admiring their new silver epergne

Fancy-dress party aboard R.M.S. Saxon *during Mary's honeymoon, September 1911. Mary is standing in the centre, in profile, looking to her left*

Abe's house Rust-en-Vrede, at Muizenburg, Cape Town

Mittie, Willie, Mary and Derry on the occasion of Willie's coming-of-age celebrations at Rossmore, 1913

Abe (left), and Cecil Bailey with her stepmother Mary (right) at Rust-en-Vrede, 1915

Above: *Mary (second from right) serving as a driver with the Royal Flying Corps, 1915*

Left: *38 Bryanston Square*

Below: *Abe with the Prince of Wales (the future King Edward VIII) at Grootfontein, 1926*

Dukes galore – Sutherland, Abercorn, etc., Winston, Kipling, Kylsant, Beaverbrook, Louis Greig, Jellicoe and a dozen more 'stars' ... a dinner of oysters, soup, fish, beef, quails, ham, asparagus and a savoury. Ten courses with dessert. Stout, sherry, champagne, port, madeira and three liqueurs. I did all but ham ... far too much.

Another of Abe's contemporaries wrote, 'he was about the only great political host left in England. They were magnificent occasions without garishness. Gold cups won on the turf rubbed shoulders the whole length of the table. Soup was served in silver plates. Delicacies were flown from France, if need be, to delight the guests. Every detail was studied for the pleasure of others. Even the matchboxes carried the famous black and gold racing colours and the host's monogram.' What this writer doesn't say is that Abe also had footmen in livery standing behind the chairs. He had three permanent footmen and a butler, and for some dinners he brought in extra waiters from Searcy's in tailcoats. Even so, this was not excessively grand by the standards of the great houses of London in those years.

In the meantime, Abe's political life in South Africa had been going through vicissitudes. He had represented Krugersdorp for the Unionist party in the Transvaal parliament from 1908 until 1910, when he stood for the same seat in the newly created Union of South Africa parliament. But in 1910 his party did not feel confident that he was a true Unionist: he seemed to have too much sympathy for their opponents, the South African Party, led by his erstwhile enemies Botha and Smuts. So he was not elected to the new parliament that he had done so much to bring about. His Unionist detractors were right: he had sympathy for the Boer point of view, which made it impossible for him to sit as a Unionist again.

People in South Africa thought that after his defeat in the election of 1910 he might leave South Africa altogether. And for a year or two this did seem a possibility, although he and Mary continued to journey back and forth. Mary would have loved to leave South Africa. She enjoyed her life in England, dividing her time between Yewhurst and Bryanston Square. There are happy photographs of

Mary Ellen as a baby on the lawn at Yewhurst, and funny cartoons by Mary of her mother and herself learning to play golf. But Abe was not at ease. Ties to South Africa were too strong, and he wanted to take an active part again in shaping its future. In February 1914, while in London with Mary and his six-month-old daughter, and with a general election due in South Africa the following year, he announced that he would return in August of that year, and would remain permanently. He would contest the next election, standing as an independent, for his same constituency, and he would support Botha in his policy of bringing the Dutch and the English together.

On 31 July 1914, Abe's horse Son-in-Law won the Steward's Cup Race at Goodwood. On 28 June, one month earlier, the Archduke Ferdinand was assassinated at Sarajevo. On 4 August, the Great War began.

On 3 August, anticipating the outbreak of war and without making time to say goodbye to Mary, who was at Yewhurst, Abe travelled to Southampton to board ship for South Africa. Mary kept the two telegrams he sent her that day. The first simply said:

Goodbye Mary sorry no time to write much love Abe.

The second, sent later that day from Southampton, said:

Will take 24 days unable send message or write as we touch nowhere love to all please inform others Abe.

Was he not able to telephone her? Had their relationship by then become so stormy that he wasn't able to have a rational conversation with her? Or did she so hate the thought of him going that he knew it would be useless to talk to her?

Abe's sudden departure was caused by his wish to help South Africa mobilize to fight the war on the British side. Before he had left London he had tried to persuade Kitchener to form a South African force to fight in Europe. When he failed to do this, he decided, although he was by then fifty, that he must go back and join the army in South Africa. When he arrived there twenty-four days later he found a rebellion had erupted. Three Afrikaner generals who had fought in the Boer War were leading an insurrection against South Africa's entry into the war on the British side. The Prime Minister, Botha, who had fought with them in the Boer War, was ruthless in his pursuit of these rebellious generals, and their efforts were thwarted. Abe was active in helping Botha. He served as Intelligence Officer, as he had before, to General Lukin, who ran the counter-campaign. After that successful operation, Abe became more active. He was made Deputy Assistant Quartermaster General to General Botha, who headed a campaign to oust the Germans from South-West Africa. The brilliant fighting skills of the South Africans brought about a swift surrender from the Germans, the first of the war.

Abe returned to England briefly before October, probably in order to persuade Mary to join him in South Africa. He was successful. In the meantime, Mary had started working to help the war effort: she and her two step-children were busy making splints for hospitals at Yewhurst, and incidentally drawing funny cartoons of each other doing it. But in October Mary, Abe, and Abe's daughter Cecil embarked on the *Saxon* again, for Cape Town. There are more funny cartoons drawn on board of Cecil and Abe playing cricket on deck, and Cecil drew some too. But Mary's own daughter was not on board. She had been left behind in England – the first of many desertions. Mary Ellen was fifteen months old, and provided with everything a baby might need – nanny, nursery maid, loving grandfather and grandmother – except her mother and father. It was something she and her future siblings were to grow used to. Jim, the second son, says he doesn't remember meeting his father until he was five or six years old, so little did their lives intersect.

Derry and Mittie kept the child and her entourage with them, whether they were at the Stud House or in Ireland. Mary was away for nearly a year – she didn't sail back to England until September 1915. Derry addressed a letter to her in Madeira two days after she sailed:

Monday night 27 September Rossmore.

My darling Mary, Oh what joy to get Abe's wire 'Mary sailed today' that was sent on 25th September – I had just written to him *the day before* saying 'please send Mary Home, I am getting an old man and want to see my daughter etc'!!! I had (on purpose) never said a word to him on the subject before – as it is generally a gt mistake to meddle – but I'd stood it *about* as long as a Daddy could! – I hear that Willie is back again in London, I fancy (but I don't *know*) that Mammie and v likely Dick knew about his coming home and purposely never told me – I don't like this for it is all wrong. – and I trust there is nothing wrong behind it – I have been frightened out of my life all day today by a letter I got from the Admiralty saying 'Lieut. Honble W Westenra sailed from Muros on Hospital ship Aquitania, reason for his going not known' – what on earth was I to make of that?

Mammie and Dick went off to London on day before yesterday Sat 25th – and arrived Sunday 26th – I can only suppose that they *knew* that Willie had arrived or was arriving – I don't think it was nice at-all and I still hope that there is nothing wrong – it is all so very *queer*.

Mary Ellen is in awf fine form and keeps on telling me that 'Mammie is coming Home' – of course she will not know her very own darling Mother when her Mother DV sees her, but you will not expect too much will you Darling, she very soon will know you and love you a whole whole lot – Oh I am so glad you are coming Home – I am trying to catch you at Madeira but I'm afraid I shall be too late – I have been so knocked about with this Admiralty letter received this morning that I cannot write (even to *you*) any more just now – and most likely you will never get it!

I am not going to allow Mary Ellen DV to leave here till *you* come and take her away – she's awf well thank God and is SO sweet to Gran*PAH* – that's the way she yowls at me! …

I *do* hope you'll get this Darling, but *Oh* how I loved Abe's wire. So glad he has given you a pearl dog collar (at first I thought it was a collar for the dog he'd given you!)

God bless my darling daughter
Loving and devoted old Daddy

In the year Mary had been away, her daughter had changed from a baby to a little girl who could talk, and who was full of excitement at the thought of seeing her mother. Derry's comment that 'she very soon will know you and love you a whole whole lot' sounds wise and gentle. It is most strange, though, that Mittie should have rushed off to London with Dick, telling Derry nothing about Willie's possibly being wounded. This letter is a revelation: of Derry's kindness; of his odd relationship with Mittie; and, above all, of his deep love and need for Mary.

Before Mary sailed, she and Abe and Cecil had their photographs taken at Rust-en-Vrede. Abe is in his army greatcoat with his Major's crown on the shoulder. Mary and Cecil, almost the same age, look soft and vulnerable in their long skirts and pale blouses. Mary has her new dog, a gift from Abe, beside her.

When the campaign against the Germans in South-West Africa was over Abe used his own money to finance a fighting unit to be sent to France. He had raised a unit – 'Bailey's Rosebuds' – in 1906, in order to help quell a Zulu uprising. In 1915, during which year he was elected to the Cape parliament as an independent, Abe suggested forming a body of first-class sharpshooters to join the British Expeditionary Force in France. Six months later, after a welter of red tape had been cut through in Whitehall, Abe's offer was accepted. Abe organized advertisements throughout South Africa for top-grade marksmen. In the end only twenty-five were good enough – and eventually twenty were sent to France. Bailey's Sharpshooters became famous for their courage and skill. Only six of Bailey's Sharpshooters survived the war. They were awarded many medals by both the French and the English, and Abe was given the Croix de Guerre and made a baronet at the end of the war in recognition of his contribution.

When Mary got back to England, she had to decide what her contribution to the war effort should be. She decided she would like to be a driver. In 1914 Abe had given her her own car – a Peugeot three-litre drophead coupé, chic and dashing. No doubt

Mary, who adored driving and had a passion for speed – she was once fined for driving at 40 m.p.h. down Pall Mall – drove it with her foot right down on the floorboard 'and the full of the clock on her', as her Monaghan neighbours might say.

Her first step was to join the Women's Legion, in 1916. In 1917 it became first the Women's Auxiliary Air Corps, and shortly after, the women's section of the Royal Flying Corps. So Mary had become connected at last to flying, which was to become the dominating interest of her life. She was not allowed to learn to fly, but she was was doing the next best thing, as a driver. She now had to learn what happened under the bonnet of cars and lorries, and how to change a wheel. She was exposed to the mechanical problems of dealing with a combustion engine. All this would help her in years to come when she had her own aeroplane.

In 1918 the R.F.C. and the Royal Naval Air Service (R.N.A.S.) were combined, and formed into the Royal Air Force, with a separate women's section, the Women's Auxiliary Air Force. This restructuring was due to the terrific growth of air power between the formation of the R.F.C. and R.N.A.S. (in 1912 and 1914, respectively), and 1918. In 1911 it was reported by the Chairman of a Defence Committee that 'at the present time we have ... of actual flying men in the army about eleven, and of actual flying men in the navy about eight, and France has about two hundred and sixty-three – so we are, what you might call, behind'. But so rapidly did the role of the aeroplane evolve during the war that it became an all-important weapon.

During Mary's time as a military driver she went to France, and was active near the fighting. She was forced to leave the R.F.C. for the birth of twins – a son, Derrick Thomas Louis Bailey (Derrick after his mother's father, Thomas after his father's father, and Louis after Louis Botha, Prime Minister of South Africa, who was probably also his godfather), and a daughter, Ann Hester Zia – on 15 August 1918.

The time she spent as part of a wartime unit suited Mary. She liked being involved in masculine exploits; enjoyed messing about with oily engines; didn't mind the discipline. Her other occupation, as mother of three young children – and soon of four, as her son Jim was born in 1919 – didn't appeal to her as much. And she didn't enjoy being Abe's hostess in Bryanston Square, even though such important events were happening there. For instance, in 1916 Abe was able to arrange a meeting between Asquith and Lloyd George in Bryanston Square, at which Asquith was persuaded to step down and let Lloyd George become Prime Minister. Abe was also able to persuade Lloyd George to have Winston Churchill in his cabinet. On the eve of the Bryanston Square meeting he wrote to Lloyd George: 'I only hope to God everything goes right and you are elected P.M. Then there is a chance. I shall be awfully sorry if Winston's brains and push have to be left on the shelf, for I know, and so do you, that he is full of ideas and good ones too. I have no friendship except for the Empire, and it is having these feelings that I shall for one deplore the loss of his valuable services. He will, I know, assist you in any case.'

Mary was supposed to be Abe's hostess at the mixed dinner parties he gave, but she didn't enjoy entertaining people for political or business motives, and was uncooperative and maddeningly unpunctual. Abe himself was the most punctual of men, and so his temper often flared up. He had a very short fuse. Shortly after his successful meeting with Asquith and Lloyd George, Abe struck a man in the parliamentary chamber in South Africa. When a Nationalist M.P. named F.W. Beyers made a violent verbal attack on General Botha, Abe lost his temper and punched him on the jaw. Later he apologized. 'I am ashamed and annoyed to have forgotten myself,' he said to the house.

Mary's children remember her own bad temper, which grew worse as the years went on. The two younger ones had an easier time but remember the severe beatings she gave the older children. And they remember her rages with servants. Abe often had to act as peacemaker after these domestic storms, trying to lessen the frightening effects of Mary's fury. Jim recalls that when his parents quarrelled with each other it was like 'two dinosaurs thrashing down forests with their tails' – a terrifying spectacle for a child. But outwardly the marriage hung together, and there were plenty of times of affection, and of mutual respect. A speech Abe made at this time was stuck in an album with 'Marvellous speech by Abe' written under it by Mary: she admired him through all the storms. And her children remember happy times with her, when she read to them for hours in the nursery, and she was always interested in their outdoor activities. On the whole, though, small children didn't interest her. And, as an outdoor person, living in London didn't suit her either.

By 1919 her life had fallen into a predictable pattern. Most of it was lived in Bryanston Square. The children, when they grew old enough, were taught to ride in Rotten Row, in Hyde Park, along with other privileged and nannied children. Desmond Leslie remembers being taught to ride with the Bailey children by Mrs Stuckle and recalls exchanging boasts with them about the enormous castles they each said they owned in Ireland.

Abe, who after the Great War spent more time in South Africa than in England, came back for the racing season in June and the shooting seasons. His racehorses were immensely successful. Son-in-Law and Foxlaw were two of his greatest winners, and he had fine paintings done of them by Sir Alfred Munnings. He owned stables at Newmarket, and his trainer was Reggie Day. But he was able to race throughout the year as he owned the largest and best stables in South Africa, on his Clewer estate in the Karoo.

In July Mary and the children were either in Ireland staying at Rossmore, or in a rented house at Frinton-on-Sea. In August Abe and Mary were shooting grouse, and in October, pheasants.

But how did she feel, at twenty-eight, married to a man of fifty-four? Was she regretting the bargain her parents made, gritting her teeth and getting on with it? Did she sometimes dream about what might have been? Her photograph albums show one private interest which had persisted since her childhood: Tubby Alexander, who was later to become Field Marshal Earl Alexander of Tunis. She stuck masses of photographs and cuttings of him into her books. Tubby was almost exactly Mary's age, and had had an identical upbringing in Ireland on a nearby estate. He was part of her real world – of the world she dreamt about and yearned for. In 1918 she asked him to be godfather to her daughter Ann, and he accepted. She kept his letter, written just after the christening, which he could not attend, as he was still in France. The letter is racy, funny, and full of cartoons much like the ones she drew herself. It is not in the least romantic, but it shows a jolly rollicking sort of friendship. He wrote it on 7 December 1918, twenty-six days after the end of the war.

Dec 7th

Dear Mary

I hope the christening went off well and was a great success. It's almost unbelievable to think the War is over, it seems as if we had been fighting all our lives – I shall feel awfully brave in any future drunken brawls.

It's most delicious to wander over old trenches and battlegrounds that one spent months in, hardly daring to look over the top, and now we can stroll about in perfect security.

[Here Tubby made two drawings, one of a terrified soldier in a trench and one of a cane-swinging soldier beside a trench with a cheerful sun shining.]

Very enterprising of Willie to go off to the Mumian[?] coast – I should rather like to go to Russia too – I don't think we shall have much fun here now, and I'm sure England must be pretty dull.

I can't make up my mind what to do. At present we are teaching a certain amount of civil education – reading, writing, arithmetic and so on – we had a general knowledge paper the other day – some of the answers were too funny for words. One question was the capital of Italy to which the answer was Vienna! Female for Fox – answer Foxess! I can't tell you some of the funniest!

I hear Lionel Leslie [Shane's brother] has come into the Irish Guards – I haven't seen him since he was a funny little fat thing – I wonder what he's like now – enormous I should think. Well I must end now as I'm bussy [sic] studying German, that will be useful when we get there.

My best love to my Goddaughter

Yrs aff

Tubby

[There is a drawing of a British officer saying 'Haben Sie

ein Stücktisch etc.' to a small, mustachioed, pipe-smoking German who is answering, 'I understand not ze Englisch!']

If Mary did wistfully wonder in 1918 about what might have been, she would never have discussed it. She was becoming formidable: a strong woman with a huge laugh, smoking incessantly, and with a somewhat masculine mind, even though her looks were feminine.

By 1921 her family was complete. Her second son, James Richard Abe, had been born in 1919, and in 1921 her youngest child, Noreen Helen Rosemary, was born. These two were to be her favourite children.

Also in 1921, Derry died. Apart from Abe, he was the person who had shown her most love and affection in her life. It was an extremely sad time for her, and there was little comfort to be found in her relationship with her mother. The relationship had always been stormy. There is strange evidence of this in Mary's photograph albums: two photographs of Mittie which have had their faces viciously scratched out. One is of a group on the steps of a country house in Ireland. Mittie is sitting beside Lord Cadogan, with her face obliterated. The second photograph is of Mittie in her court dress and regalia, her tiara and magnificent necklace, and a scratched-out face. Under this defaced picture Mary has written 'The Dowager Lady Rossmore, Mittie'. Which came first, the writing or the scratching out? Either way, it is disturbing. Jim remembers that his grandmother very seldom came to Bryanston Square, and there is no record of her ever going to South Africa. On the other hand, she was responsible for the children when Mary was away, and they remember often having to stay with her at the Stud House.

Mary herself spent some time in South Africa during these years. In 1923 she was at the opening of Parliament, in the great parliamentary building designed by Sir Herbert Baker in Pretoria. In 1926 she was there again, to act as Abe's hostess when he entertained the young Prince of Wales who was later, briefly, King Edward VIII. Mary had often hunted, with her Aunt Doods in Northamptonshire, on the same days as the Prince of Wales, and he would often have met Abe racing. Abe invited him to stay and shoot springbok at Grootfontein, his principal farm on his Clewer estate in the Karoo, and was delighted when he accepted. The prince was a popular, attractive figure, always the centre of romantic speculation.

Abe wanted the prince to see his extensive farms in the Karoo. He was by far the biggest landowner in what was then thought of as an unproductive wasteland. He wanted to show off his herds of merino sheep and Hereford cattle, and his famed racing stables. He had ample time to prepare munificently for the royal arrival. In time-honoured fashion, dating back to visits to great houses by good Queen Bess, Abe decided that he had to build another wing to his house. It held four more bedrooms and two more bathrooms – a huge high-ceilinged bedroom and bathroom on the ground floor for the prince and more room above for his personal bodyguards and private secretary. Above the prince's bedroom was a large water tank. The day before he was due to arrive the tank was filled for the first time. Because the building had been finished in a hurry the tank was not properly fixed to its stanchion, and when it was filled it broke loose and crashed into the prince's bedroom below. The prince had to make do with a bedroom in the old wing, but he stayed nevertheless for several days, shooting springbok and riding in the veldt on a horse called Critic. He liked the horse so much that Abe later sent it up by rail to Rhodesia so that the prince could ride it during his time there. After this Abe often met the prince in London. He was frequently invited to St James's Palace, and the prince often dined in Bryanston Square.

Mary's photograph album records her peregrinations between the wars, either with the children or without: to Monaghan; their visits to the seaside; a visit one summer with four of her children and Abe to stay at Cliveden with Nancy Astor. There are also pictures of Abe's racing triumphs at Epsom, Goodwood and Newmarket. In 1927 Abe's horse Foxlaw won the Ascot Gold Cup. But before this great event in Abe's sporting life, a momentous step had been taken by Mary in her own sporting life. In 1926, she decided she would learn to fly.

8

Getting Away from Prams

At the beginning of 1926, Mary's children were nearly all old enough to be parcelled off to boarding school. The two boys, Derrick and Jim, found themselves at a preparatory school called Edgertons, in Wixenford, no longer in existence. It was run by a headmaster who took such delight in beating his charges that fewer and fewer were sent back each term. So few boys were left by Jim's time that he found himself captaining most of the sports teams. Later both boys went to Winchester. The girls were sent, at very young ages, to St James's girls' school in Malvern, Worcestershire. Noreen, the youngest, was for a while the only child left in Bryanston Square, looked after by her beloved nursery maid Ada. But all too soon she was sent to join her sisters in Malvern. Anne was the youngest girl in the school until Noreen, three years younger, arrived.

Abe, apparently, did not object. He remembered his own childhood, when he was sent halfway across the world to get his schooling at the age of eight. Mary obviously forgot her own hatred of boarding school. She had found a new all-consuming passion, which needed all her attention.

In 1925 amateur aviation was in its infancy. Geoffrey de Havilland had produced his first light aeroplane in 1923: the Humming Bird, a single-seater powered by a converted motorcycle engine, designed to take part in gliding races. Most of his work up until then had been connected, after his first aeroplane made its one flight with him as pilot in 1909, with military aeroplanes he designed for the Royal Aircraft factory. As soon as the Great War began, he was involved in designing fighters, bombers, and reconnaissance planes, and at the end of the war he was awarded the Air Force Cross for his tremendous contribution to British air power. After the war, he was involved in designing freight and passenger planes – commercial airliners to fly to Europe, carrying eight passengers.

The first flight of the prototype De Havilland D.H. 60 Moth took place on 22 February 1925. It was a small two-seater biplane, and it revolutionized private and club flying. This was the plane in which Mary learned to fly.

In May 1925, Alan Cobham, who had already gripped the public's imagination by flying a larger De Havilland plane (the D.H. 50) to India and back the year before, flew the D.H. 60 to Zurich and back in a single day. In July of that year de Havilland delivered the first of these planes to a flying club – one of many springing up all over the country – for the use of its members. Probably the most exciting flight for Mary that year was Alan Cobham's in November, when, with an engineer and a cinematographer, he set out for Cape Town. They flew in the D.H. 50 four-seater biplane, and arrived in Cape Town on 17 February 1926. They were back in England on 13 March. Although the trio's journey took longer than any Union Castle passenger ship, the films they brought back and the accounts of their adventures thrilled the world.

This was going on at a time when there didn't seem much need for Mary in the life she led. She was uninterested in being a hostess. She had sent her children away to school, and the holidays were few and far between – there was no coming home for weekends or half terms in those days. She was not really needed for the holidays either; plenty of people were organized to look after the children and keep them entertained, although she did go with them for their annual month at the seaside. The only way in which she was remotely of interest to anyone, she felt, was as Abe Bailey's wife. Abe was famous and respected in his own right; she wasn't. She was standing two paces behind him, in his shadow. If people came to the house while he was there it was Abe that they wanted to talk to. Mary was the apparently sweet little wife in the background. But she was anything but the sweet little wife, and disliked her background position. She was, in her own mind, a courageous adventurer, longing for ways of proving her worth to herself and to other people. Domesticity and child-rearing were not what she wanted or needed.

Another underlying source of frustration might have been her husband's wealth. There was no need for her to lift the smallest finger for herself. Anything on earth that she wanted could be provided. Wealth of that sort could have a deadening effect on someone with no particular aim or ambition in life. Possessions were not enough.

Her old happy life in Monaghan was lost to her forever. Her brother William had inherited the title and the castle, and by 1923 had met the person whom he was later to marry: Dolores Cecil Lee, the divorced wife of an army officer. Mary did not get on with her, and seldom went back to Rossmore after their marriage in 1927. She did still hunt with her Aunt Doods in Northamptonshire, but she badly needed a new challenge.

Geoffrey de Havilland and his workshops at Stag Lane were in the news because of Alan Cobham's spectacular flights. It was simple for Mary to find out that the headquarters of the London Aeroplane Club was at Stag Lane, and that this club hired out planes to people for twenty shillings an hour and arranged lessons at thirty shillings an hour. In order to gain a pilot's licence one needed ten hours' flying time, spread over twenty lessons. The instructors in 1926 were Captain F.G.M. Sparkes, and his assistant, S.L.F. St Barbe. Mary started taking lessons secretly, not wanting to tell Abe she was learning to fly until she knew herself whether she was able to do it or not. She felt sure he would try to stop her if he knew.

As well as being the year when Mary started flying, 1926 was the year of the General Strike in Britain. Abe was involved in the negotiations that brought it to an end. He was not only a close friend of Winston Churchill, who at that time was Chancellor of the Exchequer in Baldwin's government, but also of Ramsay MacDonald, who had been the previous Prime Minister and was then the Leader of the Opposition. Another good friend was Jimmy

Thomas, a Labour M.P. who as a trade union leader had organized railway strikes in 1911 and 1919. The General Strike was called by the Trade Union Council as a protest against lower wages. As a result two million men went out on strike on 3 May, and the country was nearly brought to a standstill. The government put the armed forces into action, civilians volunteered to help, and all sorts of unlikely people found themselves acting as engine drivers and bus conductors and thoroughly enjoying themselves. Abe, in his usual behind-the-scenes way, arranged meetings in Bryanston Square between Thomas and Churchill and then between Churchill and MacDonald. As a result, they found a means of calling off the strike after nine days. Abe's reputation as a negotiator grew.

For Mary, the air became the element in which she felt most at home, most in control, most herself. It was an elixir which she drank greedily and with single-minded passion. On 18 October 1926 she gained her 'A' licence, which entitled her to pilot an aeroplane by herself. When she had the licence she felt able to tell Abe what she was doing; now she wanted to own her own aeroplane, and he would have to buy it. We don't know what Abe's reaction was when he heard the news, but she got her aeroplane, which would have cost between £500 and £600. The plane she bought was the De Havilland Moth D.H. 60, with a Cirrus engine: the registration number was G-EBPU and her first flight in it was on 21 February 1927. She always called the plane 'PU', and it took the role of all her favourite hunters and dogs rolled into one. She 'dromed' it, as the expression was, at Stag Lane; and Stag Lane was the aerodrome which saw the start and finish of all the important journeys she made out of England. Geoffrey de Havilland became her *éminence grise*, and his wife Louie her friend and accomplice.

As a woman with a pilot's licence in 1926, Mary was a rarity. She was asked in 1930 to write an article about women pilots, and in it she quoted a list of the women who had become pilots in England since 1911. By 1922, only nine women had gained licences. In 1925, only one woman qualified. In 1926, two women qualified – Mary and another Irishwoman, Miss Sicele O'Brien. In the following three years more women qualified: flying had become a fashionable sport for the 'gay young things' of the twenties, and by the end of 1929 forty-three more were added to the list. But in 1926 they were few and far between.

The woman who qualified the year before Mary was also Irish: Sophia Teresa Catherine Mary Eliott-Lynn, born Peirce-Evans in Co. Limerick in 1896, and so six years younger than Mary. She was the epitome of a 'bright young thing' herself – cheerful, flashy, elegant, and fond of publicity: the opposite of Mary in every way. So much attention did she seek and get when she was flying as Mrs Eliott-Lynn that the press christened her 'hell-of-a-din'. She married again at the height of her career, and became even more renowned as Lady Heath.

Mary's first flight was in Mrs Eliott-Lynn's plane, on 7 June 1926. From then on her lessons at Stag Lane were either with Mrs Eliott-Lynn or with Captain Sparkes. The following year the two women were often flying in the same plane together, or competing against each other as friendly rivals.

The moment Mary had her licence she began to compete in races, and test her skills in every way that she could. Remarkably quickly she was setting records and winning prizes. The first press coverage of her flying reports her visit to an air show in Norwich in February 1927. There is a photograph in *Flight* magazine of Mary at the Norwich event. The caption is: 'CAMERA SHY. Lady Bailey, who flew in her Moth to Norwich through very bad weather, refuses to be "took".' This was typical of Mary as she became more well known. The event in Norwich was an Aerial Rally, organized by the Lord Mayor to inspire citizens to form their own local flying club. In spite of appalling weather there were no mishaps.

In April, Mary herself had a very serious accident. Geoffrey de Havilland describes it in his book *Sky Fever*:

> She started her engine one day at Stag Lane by swinging the propeller the usual way and slipped forward on the wet grass. The result of this sort of miscalculation was often fatal, but Lady Bailey was only scalped. I happened to be there at the time and retrieved a large patch of skin and hair from the ground; and I believe it was later cleaned and bound into

place. When I next saw her she was wearing a sort of turban; but this did not prevent her from flying.

In spite of this gruesome injury Mary appeared at Bournemouth for a meeting later the same month, with her head bound in the turban, which she went on wearing for the rest of the year. But there are photographs of her the following year with nothing covering her head, and her hair looks perfectly all right, so the piece of scalp so obligingly collected by Geoffrey de Havilland must have settled back into place. Her children believe, however, that so great a blow to her head might have contributed to the deterioration of her temper and her inability to control her outbursts – which sadly became the characteristics that anyone who knew her well remembers. The accident did nothing, however, to discourage her from flying – nor did the disastrous crashes at another meeting in Bournemouth six weeks after the previous one she had attended.

Before the first race of the meeting in Bournemouth, a Major Harold Hemmings stalled his De Havilland 37 at sixty feet, hit a steel number-board and crashed. Both he and his passenger Claude Plevins were badly injured, and Plevins later died in hospital. But, in keeping with Royal Air Force tradition, racing continued. The second race was a Ladies' Race, between Mrs Eliott-Lynn, Miss O'Brien and Mary. *Flight* magazine reported that 'all three handled their machines excellently, making very good turns at the aerodrome turning point, those of Mrs. Eliott-Lynn being particularly good, and practically vertical'. She won, Miss O'Brien was second, and Mary was third.

As the next day was Sunday there was no racing, but on Monday afternoon the first race of the afternoon was a 'Medium Power Handicap'. Mary and eleven other pilots took part. Mary was the fifth to take off, which meant that there were four pilots who had a lesser handicap than she did. The planes were uncomfortably close together at one point. On the second lap, according to *Flight*, 'disaster, swift and complete, overtook two of the pilots ... those who happened at the time to be looking towards one of the field turning points, suddenly saw a machine tilt over, dive, and disappear behind the trees. That a collision had occurred was evident, but the distance was too great to make out the identity of the machines involved.'

For some agonizing minutes it seemed as if Mary's plane might have been involved. Eventually Captain Sparkes returned to the start and named the two unfortunate pilots. Both lost their lives. Three deaths, in two days of sport: no wonder Abe was terrified every time Mary went up in the air. But it didn't stop her.

Her next escapade that year was a forced landing in a field. *Flight* reported it:

> Lady Bailey, who flies nearly every day in her Moth, was flying over Leicestershire recently when engine trouble developed, and a forced landing became imperative. This she accomplished very skillfully in a field near Peatling Hall, the home of Colonel Gemmell, where she remained for the night.

Much later this incident was remembered by a fellow pilot, who wrote that 'she appeared at the door of Peatling Hall as coolly as if she had just dropped in for the hunting'.

She had found her métier. Flying was a combination of so many different elements: challenge, escape, skill – and then the sheer wonder of being carried up from the earth into the air, where the pilot's destiny lies entirely in her own hands. Yeats described it for his Irish Airman:

> A lonely impulse of delight
> Led to this tumult in the clouds.

Mary was not a poet. But her descriptions later of her feelings when flying over Africa show her total joy in the sensations of freedom and space, and disconnectedness from the earth and its problems. Laconically, she told friends 'I do it to get away from prams.' The truth was that she had become hooked. Flying was her drug, and her fascination with it lasted all her life.

The year 1927 saw a number of 'firsts' in aviation, and several were achieved by Mary. On 2 June, she was a passenger when Mrs

Eliott-Lynn set an all-time light plane (1st category) two-seater altitude record of 16,000 feet. A month later, on 5 July, Mary, flying Geoffrey de Havilland's Moth with his wife Louie as her passenger, exceeded the record by flying to 17,283 feet. In October Mrs Eliott-Lynn (now Lady Heath) almost took it from her again. She achieved a height judged to be exactly equal to Mary's; for a record she would have had to exceed it by at least a hundred metres.

This was only one of Mary's triumphs in 1927. That year she became the first woman to obtain her blind-flying certificate. For this she was required to fly in a hooded cockpit, relying entirely on the instruments in front of her – which often creates a terrible sense of disorientation, and a belief that the instruments must be wrong. In July of that year, flying in the Birmingham Air Pageant, Mary won a handicap race, flying against thirteen male competitors. In August, she decided to fly on her own across the Irish Sea. The most likely explanation for the trip is that she wanted to attend the Dublin Horse Show, in those days the most important social event in Ireland, taking place in the first week of August. Mary set off from Stag Lane in her little Moth. It was her first sea-crossing, and she took precautions: an inflatable inner tube for a motor-car tyre was pushed in amongst her luggage, in case she found herself having to swim for it. But she arrived safely in Dublin, becoming the first woman to fly solo across the Irish Sea.

Later in August, back from Ireland, she was the only woman to compete in the King's Cup race round England. At the end of it she was besieged by autograph-hunters. She competed in this exhausting race several more times – in 1929, '30, '31 and '33. In 1929 and '30 she was flying a Moth Coupe G-AAEE, and in 1931 and '33 in a Puss Moth G-AAYA.

She came second in several important races in August – the Air League Challenge Cup and two races in Nottingham. August was the month her children were all on holiday at the seaside. That year they can't have seen much of their mother: she was far too busy competing in races all over the country.

On 1 September Mary performed a special ceremony. A fellow-pilot of De Havilland Moths, Lieutenant Dick Bentley of the South African Air Force, had decided he wished to attempt a solo flight from London to Cape Town. He had persuaded a South African newspaper, the *Johannesburg Star*, to buy him an aeroplane, and Sir Charles Wakefield, the head of Shell Oil, had guaranteed him a supply of fuel. Bentley invited Mary to perform the christening ceremony for his plane. It was to be called 'Dorys', after the girl he was going to marry when he got to South Africa.

Bentley took off on his marathon flight that same morning, and arrived in Cape Town on 28 September, exactly four weeks later. This was longer than he anticipated, but was still a record. He duly married Dorys. Luckily she was an intrepid flyer herself, and a few months later, when they were flying over the Victoria Falls together, they suddenly decided that they would keep on flying until they got back to England. It was to be their honeymoon flight. It took them three months altogether, because they were distracted on the way. In Egypt, Bentley had to go to the rescue of two damsels in distress. One was Lady Heath, and the other was Lady Bailey. That was all to happen in 1928, when the two ladies were making epic flights of their own.

While Mary triumphed in the air, Abe was winning races on the ground. His horse Son and Heir came third that year in the St Leger, and Roman Market won the Tattersall's Sales Stakes at Doncaster. Did Mary witness his triumphs? Did Abe see Mary being presented with her trophies? It is doubtful, in both cases. But the collection of silver and gold cups was mounting, from both directions, on the dining-room table in Bryanston Square.

October found Mary presiding as President of the Suffolk and Eastern Counties Light Aeroplane Club. One of her duties was to help with the joyrides being given to the spectators. Her first passenger was Lord Huntingfield, who became a great friend. He served as Member of Parliament for East Suffolk from 1923 to 1929, and he was also a flying enthusiast.

On 14 January 1928 an article appeared in Abe's London magazine *The African World* headed:

'HONOUR FOR LADY BAILEY'
World's Champion Aviator

Paris, Friday

British Airmen are pressing the claims of Lady (Abe) Bailey to the title of champion woman aviator of the world. The title is to be awarded for the first time by the International League of Aviators.

There is said to be every indication that the title will be awarded to Lady Bailey instead of to Miss Ruth Elder, Mme. Lillie Deillenz, the Viennese actress, or to some other woman aviator who took part in recent flights.

Lady Bailey is being singled out, it is said, because she actually piloted her machine in her notable flights, while other women aviators have for the most part travelled as passengers.

And on 18 January, an article in the *Rand Daily Mail* proclaimed:

Lady Bailey, whom the International Union of Aviators has awarded the title of Champion Lady Aviator of the world, asks me to convey through the *Rand Daily Mail* a message of good luck to South African Flyers. In the course of an interview today she said: 'I have always been keen on flying, and I have looked upon my aeroplane as any private person does on a car – the best and quickest way of getting about. I took out my pilot's licence in 1926, and did a lot of flying last year. I keep the Moth garaged at Edgeware, and when I feel like a run I fly where I want to, sometimes with a passenger, but mostly alone. I love piloting my own machine. I think women will use aeroplanes increasingly in place of cars.'

All this was before Mary's epoch-making flight from London to Cape Town, which she began two months later, on 9 March 1928.

9

The Flight from London
to Cape Town

There is no question of trying to put up new records or
racing against the clock. I am just trying to blaze a trail that
will, I hope, be a rough guide to those in whose hands the
future of commercial flying is vested.

So Mary explained to a reporter her reasons for setting out on
her great lone journey from London to Cape Town in March
1928. She went on: 'My trip is in the nature of a rest cure. I have
felt the need of a change of scene and interest lately. I'm taking
only two suitcases, and I will renew supplies at various places of
call. I hope to be able to show that it is possible for a woman to
make journeys of this kind with less nervous strain than is involved
in a motor trip on crowded roads.'

I have felt the need for a change of scene and interest lately. How
understated, but how significant. Life at Bryanston Square, small
children, big dinner parties, Abe's preoccupation with business and
South Africa: it all amounted to boring routine. Even the races and
dashes up and down the country to different air displays and events
were not enough to dispel her feelings of uselessness and depres-
sion. Challenge on a much more demanding scale was needed.

Geoffrey de Havilland was her confidant and guide as she made
her plans. He advised her that she would not be able to fly her own
Moth 'PU', but would need the newest Moth – the X type.
Because she needed it in a hurry, he generously decided he would
sell her his own machine. It had to be adapted for her needs on the

long journey, and the work had to be done speedily and secretly, so that she could get away without too much publicity and fuss.

'Everyone concerned worked like anything, preparing this Moth for the trip, and I'm sure I was most grateful to them,' Mary wrote later, 'knowing how little I knew about the aeroplane or the engine or the rigging or the flying, on a trip like this.'

It seems extraordinary that everyone allowed her to go. It can only have been because no one could dissuade her once she had made up her mind. Geoffrey de Havilland did what he could for her. An extra fuel tank was fitted in the front cockpit, to allow her non-stop flights of up to ten hours. Otherwise, she had her instrument panel, with a compass that did not work very well, and a collection of maps that were inadequate to say the least. Some came from the Union Castle Shipping Company. Mary described it in her own unpublished account of the journey: 'I had two pages of the Union Castle Co's map book … but as this measured, with the margins and all, a total of about 5 inches long by about 3 inches wide, and showed an enormous amount of another part of the continent of Africa, also condensed into the same page … it did not show me much … Still, it worked all right.'

Apart from the reluctant sponsorship of her husband Abe, who funded her adventure, and the backing of Geoffrey de Havilland, there was a third important man whose help was invaluable to her in planning her journey. This was Sir Charles Cheers Wakefield, who had been Lord Mayor of London in 1916, and was the director of the firm of C.C. Wakefield and Co., which manufactured and distributed Castrol lubricating oils and greases. He was known as the patron saint of aviation. When Sir Alan Cobham in 1927 embarked on his 'Flight of Survey Round Africa', Wakefield was responsible for supplying over forty stations with 'everything necessary to keep Cobham on the wing'. These supplies were likely still to be available to Mary, if she chose to follow Cobham's route. It was one of the few things she could rely on as she set out, so ill-prepared, on her astonishing enterprise.

At 12.30 p.m. on Friday 9 March 1928, Mary took off, in her 80 h.p. DH 60 Moth, with its Cirrus engine, and registration code EBSF, from Stag Lane, north of London. Only Louie de Havilland

and a few mechanics were there to see her take off on that cold, rainy afternoon. Her first stop had to be Croydon, south of London: the official taking-off place for historic attempts at long-distance flights. By the time she reached Croydon it was snowing. More friends and family were there, to see the official start of her journey. Abe was in Cape Town, and the reason she gave for deciding to fly was to visit him.

She wore Russian flying boots, a flying helmet, a leather coat and a sensible skirt. The rest of her clothes were stowed in two small suitcases behind the cockpit. It was essential that she should carry as little weight as possible, as she had an extra fuel tank on board. In any case, she was not remotely concerned about her appearance, and if necessary, more clothes could be bought en route.

She sat in the back cockpit – the front one held the fuel tank – and there was no protective canopy; the cockpit was open to all weathers. In March, in snow, it must have been perishingly cold. As it was a biplane, there was the protection of the overhead wing to shield her from strong sun coming from the front of the aircraft, but it was little protection against driving wind and snow; and the windscreen in front of her was only a few inches higher than the wall of the cockpit. She wore goggles and heavy gloves, and never once complained of cold or discomfort, only of bad flying conditions.

She landed in Lympne, Hampshire, at 3 p.m. before crossing the channel; at 4.30 she landed in Berck-sur-Mer. The weather was bad – there was a thick band of fog – and Mary landed at Sacy-le-Petit instead of flying on to Lyons, her intended destination. She discovered that her compass, which she didn't completely understand, was faulty. (Harold Penrose, the aviation writer, said of her that she had left Croydon 'sublimely unaware of the function of the verge wing on her compass'.) She spent the night in Sacy, leaving at 9.30 the next morning en route for Lyons, but thick fog again prevented her, and she decided instead to land at Le Bourget, on the outskirts of Paris, which she reached at 10 a.m. on Saturday 10 March. The French press were there to meet her. They were intrigued by this intrepid thirty-eight-year-old woman, mother of five, with her ambition to set new aviation records, and they affectionately christened her 'Lady Billy'. From the moment of her arrival at le Bourget until her final arrival in Cape Town her progress was reported in all the French newspapers, as of course it was in the English and South African newspapers.

She spent the night in Paris, and had her compass adjusted – but that didn't help her to understand it any better. Then, at 9.45 a.m. on Sunday 11 March, she set off again for Lyons. She managed it this time, arriving there four and a half hours later. The weather conditions were appalling: when she arrived, a Mistral had started to blow. People warned her that she should not fly on, but, having landed at Lyons at 2.10, she insisted on taking off again at 3.30 the same afternoon. She had decided that as the wind was blowing south it would help her on – and after a tremendous buffeting she reached Marseilles at 5.30, and stayed the night.

So far, so good. Three nights spent in France, and, according to her logbook, ten hours and forty minutes of flying time since she left Stag Lane.

By Monday morning, although the Mistral had died down, the excitement in France about this lone woman's exploit had not. Not only were the press at Marignane, the airport at Marseilles, but several local pilots wheeled out their planes, and when she took off at 11.35 that morning into a cloudless Mediterranean sky she was accompanied by a skein of French pilots, dipping and bobbing around her as she left the coast and set off towards Italy.

After the hazards of the night before, the flight to Pisa must have been the first moment when Mary could really savour the joy of what she was doing. She was flying over the Gulf of Genoa – the mountains of Corsica on her starboard side, small fishing boats below her on a brilliantly blue sea, the waves sparkling, and the Moth's engine droning along companionably. Soon the Italian coast appeared, a long low misty line ahead of her, and then the mediaeval city of Pisa spread out its streets and churches for her inspection. She reached Pisa at 3.35 in the afternoon, and decided to spend the rest of the day there, exploring the city, before taking off for Rome the next morning. She was in no hurry to reach Cape Town. She was not trying to break a speed record – only to prove that such a flight was possible for a woman on her own. Part of her plan was a long holiday from all the perplexities of her life, and a chance to explore and discover more of the world than she had ever seen before. She was glorying in her freedom and independence.

The flight to Rome took three hours and ten minutes, down the west coast of Italy – a distance of about 170 miles. She arrived in Rome in time for lunch at the aerodrome at 1.45, and by 3.30 she was airborne again, because the weather looked threatening, and, according to her own account, it 'was not too good all the way to Naples'. But she made it all right, arriving at 5 in the evening.

What is so astonishing to contemplate now is that she had no wireless, no communication of any sort with the land or with the air-field she was heading for; no notion of what other planes might be taking off or landing there; no notion of what sort of surface she might be landing on or what unseen hazards in the way of tall trees or fences or telegraph wires she might fly into. So much was a matter of good eyesight and chance. And the matter of somewhere to stay the night – that was all clearly left to chance as well. All she had to help her were the signals sent on by the airport she had left to the one she was heading for: at least she knew that people would be looking out for her, and might raise the alarm if she didn't appear. And it was true that the airwaves were buzzing with news of her progress, wherever she came in to land. She was an object of huge curiosity in Italy in her up-to-the-minute model of the latest Moth. Binoculars were fixed to Italian eyes and Italian typewriters were pattering out the news of her whereabouts to the rest of the world.

Mary found all this interest somewhat disconcerting, but nev-ertheless with apparent imperturbability continued on her south-ern way. She stayed in Naples until just before lunchtime the next day, noting that the airfield in Naples was in an awkward setting. 'Some exciting moments getting out of Naples aerodrome,' she wrote. 'It is surrounded by high walls and trees.' She flew on towards Catania, on the island of Sicily – hoping to see Mount Etna on her way. She wrote: 'Straights [sic] of Messina bumpy like a lift. Mount Etna – wanted to see this, but machine so unsteady Mount Etna was skipping about like a young ram.' Mary's spelling wasn't brilliant. 'Sicele [sic] lovely fresh mild air very pretty. Had GOAT for dinner, put down on the menu as "Boeuf a l'Anglaise".' Dining on her own in an undistinguished Sicilian hotel, Mary must have wished she had someone to laugh with.

The next morning, Wednesday 14 March, she set off for Malta at 9.45 a.m. There was a haze over the surface of the sea, but the islands of Malta and Gozo appeared out of the mist just in time. At this point she admits 'my compass had been wrong from the start'. It was swung in Malta, and found to be 'out 20 degrees on some points' – almost the difference between S.E. and S.S.E. No wonder she nearly missed Malta – her compass would have been of no use in finding it for her.

There was a report of her progress in the *Cape Times* of 16 March 1928.

> Lady Bailey arrived at two o'clock this afternoon from Catania. The tiny Moth flew over Valletta at 1.30 p.m., and made a perfect landing at the Halir aerodrome. Lady Bailey, who looked tired but very cheerful, told me that so far the journey had been great fun. 'Everyone gets so excited when I arrive, and everyone is most kind everywhere I stop. They won't let me touch my machine, but do everything for me,' she said. She hoped to do longer stages in future … She intended to go on today to Homs on the African coast, but was advised not to by R.A.F. Officers here.
>
> Air Commodore Clark Hall met Lady Bailey on arrival. Wing Commander Cooke carried her off to lunch and another R.A.F. officer and mechanics took charge of the machine to overhaul it and oil it. A Naval officer superintended the swinging of her compass. Lady Bailey will leave tomorrow for Homs. The R.A.F. will see her half-way, and keep her on course by directional wireless. She told me she had no fixed timetable and a very elastic itinerary, but will 'turn up one day at Cape Town'.

There is one inaccuracy in the report. The only way the R.A.F. would be able to keep her on her course would be with a very loud megaphone, as she had no wireless receiver on board.

Because Malta was British, tremendous pride was taken there

in Mary's flight. When she left early the next morning three Royal Air Force seaplanes accompanied her for the first hour of her journey south. Mary had never seen seaplanes before, and marvelled at the way they landed on the sea and then took off again. 'It was an awfully pretty sight to watch from the air,' she recorded. And she missed them when they turned to fly home. 'When the escort turned back I had nothing to watch – no land – the engine humming, and a glare from the sun on the water.' She nearly fell asleep; jolted by a change in the note of the engine, she discovered she was flying straight up into the sky! She reacted swiftly, but 'when I pushed the stick forward to put the nose down level again, the compass showed me to be heading for Europe'. She had, in her dozy state, turned the plane not only upwards but 180 degrees in the wrong direction. Her next comments are prosaic:

> As the sea looked the same as before, I felt the compass must be wrong, but I knew I must not argue with it, so turned round and continued to fly in the other direction, deciding I must keep down. Then remembered a life-saving belt for wear on sea crossings was packed in the front of machine with spares and that I ought to have had it on.

What *did* she think about, when she first set off to fly across two hundred miles of open sea, with nowhere to land until she reached the shore of Libya? Only a few months later, her fellow-aviatrix Lady Heath was refused permission by the British authorities to fly alone over the Mediterranean. Mary must have somehow slipped through the net. Luckily the visibility was good and she reached sight of land. She was still disoriented, though: 'Felt I wanted a signpost to tell me if I ought to turn right or left.'

She was looking for somewhere she thought was called Cap Miserata, and commented that if it wasn't called that it ought to be. In fact the promontory to the east of Tripoli is called Misurata, and when she found it, she turned right. She commented on the coastline, 'Neither fish, birds, beasts or houses along most of it', but 'the colouring along the coast of red sand and the sea very vivid blue, and remarkably beautiful'.

She landed at Tripoli aerodrome at 11.40 a.m. on 16 March, a week after leaving London. She only stayed there long enough to refuel, and then made a series of hops back over Cap Misurata, landing first at Homs (now Al Kums), then at Sirte, east of Misurata, where she spent the night. That was an exhausting day – she had been flying for over six hours altogether – and when she arrived at Sirte at 3.40 p.m. she decided she had gone far enough, and found a little hotel where she stayed the night.

Next morning, Saturday 17 March, she left at 9 and flew for almost four hours over the Gulf of Benghazi. It was her last sea crossing on her way down. To reach Benghazi her flying time had been thirty-three and a half hours.

On Sunday 18 March she flew for nearly eight and a half hours, landing first at Sollum (or Salum) on the border between Libya and Egypt, where 'two gentlemen would hold heated discussions in Arabic across the lower part of my machine, till I thought their fists would go through the fabric'. Then on to Aboukir, where she spent the night. On Monday 19 March she flew into Heliopolis airport in Cairo and met the first serious obstacle on her journey. The British authorities in Egypt refused to give her permission to fly on down over the Sudan by herself. They insisted she should be escorted by a man.

'My Moth was put under lock and key, and the authorities looked as if they heartily wished they could do the same with me. I kept mentioning that I had insufficient luggage for a long stay' – but it was no good. The authorities were adamant. At this point the world's press bore down on Cairo, to see what would happen next. *The Times* of London reported it thus:

> The British Residence today definitely informed Lady Bailey that she would not be allowed to continue her flight to Cape Town unaccompanied. It is understood that Lord Lloyd [High Commissioner for Egypt and the Sudan], acting at Lady Bailey's urgent request, communicated again on the matter with the Governor General of the Sudan [Sir John Maffey, later Britain's envoy to Ireland during the Second World War], but that he remained obdurate. As Lady Bailey's

de Havilland Moth has accommodation only for the pilot she must have another machine to escort her, if she desires to continue her flight in it. It is understood that her machine has been locked in its shed in Heliopolis.

The *Cape Times*, on 28 March, under the sub-heading 'Safety First the Reason for the Restriction on Lady Bailey', quoted Air Vice Marshal Webb-Bowen, the Air Officer Commanding the Royal Air Force in the Middle East, who pronounced himself

> in entire agreement with the authorities who declined to allow Lady Bailey to proceed on her way south from Cairo. It was essentially not a flight, he said, to be undertaken by a single plane. Thousands of square miles of the country, on the Sudan and along the Upper Nile, were so swampy and so overgrown with impenetrable vegetation, that a forced landing anywhere there, even if one was not killed outright, could only have a fatal ending. The pilot would be hopelessly lost twenty paces from the machine.

He went on, most ungallantly, about a part of the country where the R.A.F. had bombed native tribes, saying:

> Supposing Lady Bailey were forced to land in a similar unruly spot? There could again be only one end to that. And the death in this way of a woman would, naturally, cause far more stir than a man. It would probably entail a punitive expedition costing a quarter of a million. In every respect the attitude of the authorities, however annoying it might appear to an intrepid lady, was the only wise one.

Air Vice Marshal Webb-Bowen further stated that no machine was ever permitted to set out alone from any aerodrome in Palestine, Syria, Iraq, Trans-Jordania or the Sudan. So what Mary was hoping to do was clearly out of the question.

Benjamin Bennett, in his book *Down Africa's Skyways*, is even more imaginatively graphic in his description of what might have happened to her:

The least divergence from the course, or an unchecked leak of petrol, might have made necessary a descent in the dominions of a cannibal king or a village of mysterious dwarfs. Perhaps landings would take place on an island lapped by a fierce river, or in a swamp alive with repulsive and underfed animals, or again in one of those places described by Sir H. Rider Haggard: 'Above Kosti, some 175 miles from Khartoum, there was a country of Nilotic negroes. Dinkas; many of whom are of unusually large physique, and live to the east of the Nile. They were known as a people of uncertain temper who often wore their hair cut to resemble a cock's comb, and bleached it with dung ... the snarling jackals and the roaring of man-eaters might take the place of London's rumbling shrieking traffic; and maddening heat instead of fog and sleet, torment the little Eden.'

Only three months before Mary arrived in Cairo a Captain V. Fergusson, a District Commissioner, part of the British Administration in the Sudan, was murdered by Sudanese insurgents. This resulted in harsh punitive raids by the R.A.F., which made the British overlords even more unpopular.

In spite of all the horrific warnings, Mary still wanted to go, and go by herself. Eventually wisdom prevailed and a solution was found, but not before Mary had spent a frustrating seven days in Cairo badgering officials. For diversion, she had contacts in Cairo, including Arthur Merton, the *Times* correspondent; Lord Lloyd, the High Commissioner; Group Captain and Mrs MacLean; Air Commodore Board; Flight Lieutenant and Mrs Dixon; Major and Mrs Hayley; and a good tobacconist, in the Shepherd's Hotel buildings. Mary notes in her logbook that a box of twenty-five 'Specials' will cost her eight piastres.

Eventually it was through Abe that a companion flyer was found. After receiving several agonized messages from Mary explaining her plight, Abe contacted the *Johannesburg Star*, which was sponsoring the South Africa to London flight of Dick Bentley, who was about to set out, via Khartoum and Cairo, with his new wife Dorys. Luckily they were in no hurry, because they had already been contacted by another damsel in distress, in the shape of Lady Heath, who had been told she was not allowed to fly unaccompanied across the Sudan on her solo flight to London from South Africa. Dick and Dorys had cheerfully agreed that they would be her protectors, meeting her south of the Sudan, and flying with her to Khartoum. Abe was able to arrange that after that mission of mercy, Dick and Dorys would meet Mary in Khartoum, and fly back with her as far as Malakal, on the Nile, 420 miles south.

Mary reluctantly agreed to this proposition. At least it meant that her solo flight would not be jeopardized: she would still be flying solo, even if accompanied by another plane. She had been made to sign a letter in Cairo, promising that she would not fly over the southern Sudan alone. Now her little Moth was unlocked and wheeled out onto the tarmac at Heliopolis airport.

Meanwhile, Lady Heath had met up with Dick and Dorys Bentley in Jinja, Uganda, and was proceeding towards Khartoum. She was flying a Mark III Avian with the registration number G-EBUG, and her trip was causing as much interest as Mary's. Her flight lasted from 17 February – she had started three weeks before Mary set out from Croydon – until 17 May, when she arrived back in Croydon. She was the first woman to achieve a solo flight from South Africa to England. Mary later eclipsed this record by achieving the double triumph of flying solo both ways.

On Tuesday 27 March Mary flew south along the Nile, landing first at Assuit, and next at Luxor, where she decided to stay for two nights, so that she could tour the Tombs of the Kings. She makes no comment about them in her account of the flight, but four years later, perhaps because of this experience, she volunteered to help in an archaeological survey of the Kharga Oasis, in the Egyptian desert not far west of Luxor.

Her next stop for refuelling was on Thursday 29 March, at Aswan. From there she flew down to Wadi Halfa. The *Cape Times* had this report on Saturday 31 March: 'Lady Bailey, despite great heat and adverse weather, set out from Aswan to negotiate the hazardous route to Halfa over country hard to beat for lack of landing facilities. She accomplished the flight in 125 minutes, and landed

in a howling gale and sandstorm, which rendered visibility ve
poor. It was a splendid performance. Lady Bailey is starting for
Atbara and Khartoum tomorrow.'

In her laconic way, Mary describes in her journal what happened
next, on her way from Wadi Halfa to Shereik, some 250 miles
south, on Saturday 31 March. She had to cross the great expanse of
the almost empty Nubian Desert, in northern Sudan.

> After Wadi-Halfa I had a forced landing in the desert, and
> worked there for about two hours [three, according to her
> logbook; then the machine took off and flew alright. I think
> by the look of the engine I must have put too much oil in it
> at Wadi-Halfa. There was no gap at all to the points of the
> rear magneto. The rev counter and air-speed indicator had
> ceased for good.

These were three harrowing hours working in burning heat, in an
uninhabited region, desperately trying everything to get her life-
saving machine working again. In Cape Town later that year, Mary
was approached by a journalist for the Cape Town magazine
Woman's Realm. The journalist said, 'I suppose you know your
engine thoroughly.' 'Well,' Mary replied, 'I know fairly well how to
fix things up. I suppose I should really know more about it than I
do – but if you are forced down miles away from anywhere, the
knowledge that you can't move until the engine has been set right
is sufficient incentive to make you get down to it and simply peg
away until the fault has been found and corrected.'

That is what she did in the Nubian Desert, from 10.30 a.m.
until 1.30 p.m. – three hours of desperate anxiety. Because everyone was following her flight and knew where she was heading, she
might eventually have been found and rescued if the engine had
not started – but for those two or three hours she was working
alone, at an engine she barely understood, literally for dear life.

An hour later she was safely in Shereik, where she stayed for
only half an hour, and then she flew on to Atbara, a slightly larger
settlement on the banks of the Nile, where she stayed the night,
not leaving until 2 the next afternoon, to fly down to Khartoum.

ile. 'Flying down from Cairo to Khartoum the
of cultivation on each bank looked like a green
ɣ out through the desert.' Following this green
180 miles from Atbara, the desert stretching out
er side, she eventually reached Khartoum, at ten
p̠—   ⸱day 1 April. Waiting for her there were Lieutenant
and Mrs Bentley, and Lady Heath, who later described Mary's
arrival.

> On Sunday, 1st April Lady Bailey arrived in Khartoum, after
> a very gallant and plucky flight, with a badly behaving
> engine and a forced landing in the desert. It hurt me to see
> her looking tired and weary after it. I cannot speak too highly
> of Lady Bailey's gallant and plucky attitude in making this
> flight, when she had never flown outside England before.

Later that day a dinner was given in honour of the two aviatrixes. Mary must have been all too conscious of the fact that, however she professed not to care about her appearance, she was
upstaged at the dinner by Lady Heath's appearance in an elegant
evening dress, while all Mary had to wear was the tweed suit she
flew in. But Mary's aristocratic background would have carried her
through a social situation that might have been a disaster for someone else. She would have had too much innate social confidence
to worry about whether Sophie Heath was scoring points over her
or not.

Later that year, after Lady Heath had finally got home –
although she was forbidden to fly across the Mediterranean by herself, she did in fact do it – she sadly lost her reputation with the
British public when she attempted to set up a height record under
false pretences. The Rugby Aeronautical Club had to announce,
scathingly, that the record Lady Heath claimed to have established
was 'entirely without justification'.

The press was agog at the thought of the paths of these two
remarkable aviatrixes crossing so fortuitously in Khartoum. They
were there together for four days, and on the day Mary was due to
fly down across the dangerous part of southern Sudan, she hit the

headlines again when a misdemeanour from her past came up in court from England. The whole incident, and her response to it, were typical of her.

> Lady Bailey (represented by a solicitor) was summoned at Brentford, Middlesex, for exceeding the speed limit in her motor car, and producing an expired driving licence. A policeman gave evidence that she was travelling at 48 m.p.h. in a 30-mile limit. She told him 'the road was quite clear and I cannot see what harm has been done'. Lady Bailey was fined in her absence seventy shillings.

It seems unlikely that the guilt of her crime clouded her mind as she climbed into the air on Thursday 5 April, with the Bentleys close behind her.

10

South from Khartoum

Khartoum, the capital city of the Sudan, sits on the bend where the Nile branches into the White Nile and the Blue Nile. It was the scene of the great siege of 1884–5, and of General Gordon's triumph and disaster. Some traces of that epic siege must have been there still, in 1928, for Mary to see – but her time in the city was taken up with being entertained by the large British colony of civil servants and diplomats and military people, struggling to maintain British rule over their Sudanese Condominium, and delighted to have three flying celebrities in their midst.

After four cheerful days there, with congenial companions, all with their own stories to tell of hazardous flights and funny incidents – the worst thing about flying alone for Mary must have been the lack of anyone to laugh with – she and her aeroplane were fully prepared for the second half of her journey south. There were still four thousand miles of flying to be done.

The Bentleys in their Moth, and Mary in hers, took off from Khartoum together very early in the morning of Thursday 5 April. Lady Heath flew out in the opposite direction to continue her pioneering flight back to England.

Mary had every reason to trust and admire Dick Bentley. He had already achieved the challenge she had set herself, by flying from London to the Cape in September 1927, in twenty-eight days, and so setting a new speed record for that flight. (That record was later broken by Lieutenant P. Murdoch, who in 1928 flew from England to the Cape in thirteen and a half days.) But as they set off neither pilot was worrying about records or speed: they were glorying in the sheer fun of the enterprise. The element of risk, because of the dangerous terrain they were crossing, added the needed frisson of tension and excitement.

Dorys, Dick's new wife, was the least comfortable of the three. She was crammed into the front cockpit of Dick's plane along with the extra fuel tank. But she had accepted at the start of their honeymoon journey that if she wanted to go with him this was to be her lot, and she didn't complain.

All went smoothly for the next three days. Mary and the Bentleys flew together to Malakal, stopping for the night in Kosti on the way. On 7 April they flew on to Mongalla. Soon after they took off from Mongalla on the 8th, Dick and Dorys turned their plane and flew back to Khartoum, their mission accomplished. Mary described the scene: 'Khartoum was very hot, and Kosti hotter still. From here the view of the yellow sand and the extreme loneliness of the desert began to change to grasses, scrub, marshes, rocks, dead treestumps, and finally the forest. Mr. Bentley, who had escorted me from Khartoum, left Mongalla with me and over Nimule he turned back as this had finished the southern Sudan.'

Later, in describing the journey down to a reporter in Cape Town, Mary scoffed at the fears of the authorities for her safety. It obviously still rankled that they had forced her to wait for the protection of a man to fly across southern Sudan. 'The journey was nothing like as alarming as some people believe. I found no lions, tigers and elephants, though I looked for them very carefully over large tracts of wild country.'

Incidentally, in this interview she told the reporter that she had not realized such a flight as hers, from London to Cape Town, would be possible until Lieutenant Bentley told her that it was, at the time she christened his aeroplane for him. And she made a most revealing admission. 'As soon as my husband gave his consent, I made preparations. I left my children with my mother, but did not tell her where I was going, as she would have worried.'

In her journal she described the country south of Nimule: 'The whole country from Nimule on to Kisumu was green, and had mountains and rivers – some roads, some native villages, an occasional mission station; and the country increased in beauty and habitation right up to Kisumu on Lake Victoria. Lake Victoria was immence [sic], one could only see a small part of it even from the air – the scenery and country round Kisumu looked better even from the ground than from the air.'

She continues: 'I was afraid of getting stopped again at Nairobi, and of being asked to have another escort, so I decided to fly direct to Tabora and cut Nairobi out. Otherwise I should have loved to have seen that part. I took a direction on the compass on the east side of Lake Victoria, and kept to that. I landed on a piece of ground that made an excellent landing ground at Shinyanga.'

Mary landed there because she was slightly lost again. Having discovered that Tabora was a hundred miles farther south, she took off. It was when she eventually found Tabora that disaster struck.

'I went on to Tabora, where I crashed my machine by landing upside down. It was my own fault, through ignorance of the fact that in the heat of the day at high altitudes [Tabora is 5000 feet up] the air is more rarified and necessitates landing at a greater speed.' She had never before flown over such high altitudes.

'With the machine upside down on the aerodrome I couldn't think which way to turn the cock, to turn the petrol off, as it was pouring out. But then I realised I *had* turned it off, and the petrol was pouring out of the air vent pipe. I felt rather unhappy at crashing the machine I had started in.' She drew a picture of the crash for her children.

Mary's understatement is truly amazing. She had escaped unhurt from a crash in the desert; petrol was pouring out of the machine in the hot sun; the whole plane could have caught on fire; and she was totally stranded. And she felt 'rather unhappy'.

Later the *Cape Times* enlarged on the reason for the crash:

> Lady Bailey attributes the cause of her crash at Tabora to the fact that she had no map at this stage of her journey. She had flown to Nzega (half way between Shinyanga and Tabora) but found it impossible to land, so she turned back to Shinyanga to inquire the route, and thence went to Tabora, which she reached in the hottest part of the day, when the air is bumpy. She is of the opinion that she insufficiently noticed the conditions, and struck an air pocket near the ground.

The Times of 13 April added more details from Mary's account of the crash.

> She said the machine made a heavy landing and its under-carriage collapsed. The machine turned over and came to rest upside down. The fuselage and wing spars were broken in places. It has now been dismantled and the engine and tanks have been saved. Although Lady Bailey thinks that the crash was due to her omission to remember the conditions prevailing at 2.30 p.m. at this altitude, she considers that this aerodrome could be made easier if a gap were cut in the line of trees bordering the west side, in order to facilitate approach from that direction, as it is at present difficult to get into the aerodrome during the heat of the day.

At this point the whole enterprise could have collapsed igno-miniously. Telegrams were sent north and south. To her mother, Mary telegraphed:

CRASHED AT TABORA BUT SELF ALRIGHT. LOVE MARY.

To Abe, she telegraphed:

CRASH LANDED AT TABORA. SELF UNHURT. PLANE BADLY DAM-
AGED. LOVE MARY.

Her next telegram to Abe showed that she was determined to go on. And he was to help her. What was the good of having so powerful and rich a man as a husband if he could not help her out in an emergency? She decided in her desperation to put him to the test, and cabled him, asking if it would be possible for him to make arrangements for her to continue her flight in an Air Force machine.

Abe obediently sprang into action. He contacted Colonel Pierre van Ryneveld, Director of the Union Air Force, and himself a long-distance flyer of renown. In 1920 he himself had made the flight from London to Cape Town with Flight Lieutenant Brand, and had crashed on the way, and had had to replace two aeroplanes, finally arriving in Cape Town in a third plane. It had taken him forty-four days – a record at that time. And in 1927 he was still breaking records: he had flown non-stop from Pretoria to Cape Town, 850 miles, in exactly nine hours. He was surely the most sympathetic person Abe could have appealed to.

Van Ryneveld passed Abe's request that Mary should be allowed to continue her flight in an Air Force plane to a subordinate, Colonel Cresswell, who told Abe it was contrary to government policy to lend military planes to civilians. Abe then contacted his old friend Sir Julius Jeppe, in Johannesburg, to see if he could help. Sir Julius must at once have reached for his telephone, for later in the day the Johannesburg Light Plane Air Club – the major amateur flying club in South Africa – came up with an offer of three different Moth aeroplanes, which could be flown up to Mary. The Club Instructor, Lt G.W. Bellin, offered to fly her the one she chose. Meanwhile, another offer came from Nairobi, from a Captain Mansfield, to send his own Moth to Mary. Later, Sir Julius Jeppe told Abe of another Moth, in Bulawayo, that Mary could have. All this was reported in the *Cape Times* on Friday 13 April – four days after the crash. Everyone then waited for Mary to make up her mind which she wanted.

One idea was that Lt Bellin would fly a plane to Mary, and then come back with her in the borrowed plane, as a passenger. But that idea would clearly not suit Mary at all. Her flight was solo: a passenger was out of the question. And by then Mary had definitely decided – perhaps spurred on by a sense of rivalry with Lady Heath, who was completing her solo flight the other way – that she must have her own plane, and not one that had to be given back when she got to Cape Town. She had decided she wanted to do the flight both ways, and be the first woman to do so by herself.

The cables flew back and forth. Abe gave his whole mind to it, although at the time he was not well. He even brought the Prime Minister of South Africa, General Hertzog, into it. Three days later, the *Cape Times* announced what it thought was the arrived-at solution. Major Mentjes, an officer in the S.A.A.F., was delegated to fly a Moth, bought by Abe in Johannesburg, to Mary in Tabora. He was to leave Swartkops aerodrome in Pretoria at dawn on Monday 16 April. He was to try to reach Livingstone that evening, and fly all day on Tuesday, hoping to get to Tabora that evening. He would then hand the plane over to Lady Bailey, and come back to South Africa by road and sea. Major Mentjes was also a breaker of flying records. He had recently broken Pierre van Ryneveld's record by flying from Cape Town to Pretoria in only seven hours and fifty-five minutes.

In the event he did not get to Tabora until 19 April. Mary sent a cable to Abe dated the 20th, saying

MENTJES ARRIVED YESTERDAY. GOOD GOING, HOPE TO PROCEED FRIDAY.

But this was not to be the end of Major Mentjes' trip. Mary was not happy about the quality of the aeroplane that Abe had bought her in Johannesburg. She telegraphed Geoffrey de Havilland in London to ask his advice. He was able to tell her that there was a much newer Moth, exactly like her own crashed one, in Nairobi. Major Mentjes was sent on to Nairobi, and there he was able to exchange the Johannesburg plane for the newer Moth, which he then flew back to Mary.

While Mary was waiting for all this to happen she did one or two practical things. 'We dismantled my machine and tried out the engine on some railway rails in the railway workshops, and there it seems all right. The fusilage [sic] was the only trouble as that was broken through the long cross.' She had something to watch while she was there, too. 'While I was at Tabora I watched the R.A.F. and S.A.A.F. flights pass through on their way to Khartoum.' How frustrating it must have been, explaining to her fellow flyers why she was stuck in Tabora, and watching them soar merrily off into the northern sky.

On Saturday 21 April, in her new Moth, G-EBTG, she left Tabora. In the short time between its arrival and her departure she had had it fitted with the auxiliary oil and petrol tanks from her old plane. It was six weeks since she had left London, and twelve days since the crash-landing. She was heartily sick of Tabora, and delighted to be winging south again, over the uninhabited hilly region of southern Tanganyika, down to the tip of Lake Tanganyika, where she landed four hours later, at what was then called Abercorn, and is now Mbala. She describes it: 'Abercorn is right up in the mountains, 6,000 feet up. There are no mosquitoes here. The country looked very good and the scenery and vegetation were wonderful.'

She flew on next morning to Broken Hill (now Kabwe). Here she succumbed to some sort of fever, which she said started as she was flying from Tabora. It was the first time her health had broken down. The *Cape Times* described it as 'a bad attack of influenza'. But it only held her up one day. She flew on, on Tuesday the 24th, to Livingstone, on the border of Northern and Southern Rhodesia. She saw the Victoria Falls from the air, and circled them once or twice, high enough not to be blinded by the cloud of mist, and reminding herself of the time when she and Abe had seen the falls together on their honeymoon. But there are no rhapsodic or even sentimental comments about what must be the most dumbfounding natural wonder on the continent of Africa. Her comments are only on the flying conditions. 'Then a very bumpy trip to Bulawayo, over a railway line that runs dead straight for mile after mile. This and the bumps seemed everlasting. ... Over Bulawayo one sudden bump sent my petrol funnel out of the machine past my head, but it luckily didn't fall on anyone and was recovered.'

She was greeted at Bulawayo aerodrome by the mayor and mayoress, and by Mr Bonnard, who was the representative there of Abe's company Lonrho. Finally, at Bulawayo, she got rid of the fever. After the night there, her next objective was Pretoria.

'I muddled my next trip, going to Pretoria. I picked up a new railway line that was not on my map, realised it was wrong, and as usual landed down to ask.' Then, in another village, she landed because she had run out of petrol. The villagers rushed around with buckets and jugs, collecting all the drops of petrol they could, and with this she was able to continue.

Her description of her stop at Warmbaths paints an alarming picture. 'Landed at Warm Baths with the sun going down, in a field of ant-hills.' Either here or previously at Nylstroom, the Light Aeroplane Club of Johannesburg had sent a replacement magneto, via the S.A.A.F., and they also took away a lot of her spares to make the plane lighter, so that she could get off more easily among the anthills.

She was getting nearer and nearer to her target: Cape Town. On 27 April she left Warmbaths en route for Pretoria. The S.A.A.F. decided they would send out a welcoming escort. Among the pilots, most appropriately, was a Miss Douglas, the first lady pilot of the Johannesburg Flying Club, flying solo. At Pretoria there was great rejoicing from a huge crowd assembled to meet her. She then flew on the short hop to Johannesburg the same evening and spent the night there.

She left Johannesburg at 1 p.m. on the 28th, and flew to Bloemfontein, where she stayed the night. From there she flew on to Beaufort West, arriving at 12.30 p.m., and she stayed the night there too. The last day of her flight to Cape Town is dramatic, and she describes it in a long, barely punctuated scrawl:

> I had heard about difficulties in the Hex River Mountains which had to be crossed. So I thought I'd get up very high and go over like that and have no bother. I took a lot of trouble climbing all the way to get a good height but it was all

wasted as the machine sank as I got over the mountains. Then I at last got to one big range where when I went high enough to go over the wind came so strong against that I could not make any headway and when I went lower I could advance but was too low to fly so I went off to the south over a lower bit and came back low down up to the next valley and when I climbed up again to look over the next range I saw it was the last one and I could see the top of Table Mountain sticking up out of a sea of cloud in the distance.

Table Mountain was Cape Town – Table Mountain was home and Abe. It is an extraordinary picture, this tiny open biplane, dipping and tossing above enormous mountains, with one woman on board relying only on her eyesight and common sense to prevent her from colliding with a peak or being blown against a precipice – and then, miraculously, to see her final objective, Table Mountain, jutting out of its collar of mist.

Meanwhile, at Young's Field, Wynberg, just outside Cape Town, a great assembly had been waiting since early in the day, anxiously looking into the north-eastern sky for the first sight of her. The mayor of Cape Town was there. The local flying club was there. When Mary didn't appear at the expected time, two of the local pilots decided to go up and look for her. Captain Black went up first, and searched for over an hour. Than Mr Williamson went up, and he flew as high as 5000 feet looking for her, but without any luck. People were getting anxious. 'There she is, up there trying to kill herself,' Abe was heard to murmur, 'and here am I down here trying to stay alive.'

At long last a tiny black dot appeared in the north-eastern sky. It gradually shaped itself into a midge, then a mosquito, then its engine could be faintly heard – then, tipping gently from side to side as it came down, the Moth and its pilot could be clearly seen. The landing was perfect.

There is an ancient piece of film which shows the plane first appearing and growing gradually bigger as it comes in, then landing. Then there's a break, and for a few seconds Mary is seen climbing down from the cockpit and cramming her big-brimmed felt hat on top of her flying helmet, and walking smiling towards the camera. But as recorded in still photographs, the actual sequence of events was slightly different. Mary climbed out of the cockpit and Abe was the first person to greet her. He kissed her cheek, and the newspapers reported that she said: 'Hello Abe, how are you? I'm a bit late – I got muddled up in the mountains'. Then she saw the army of photographers and cine-cameramen advancing on her, and she said, as they begged her to pose for photographs, 'Let me get my old hat on first.' Then she climbed back into the plane, got the hat, and crammed it on over her flying helmet. Then more photographs were taken. The later photographs show Abe standing beside her looking as proud as a mother hen with sixteen chicks, and Mary looking radiantly happy, both with wonderful smiles. She is looking tidy and elegant too, in a becoming loose striped jersey and woollen skirt. All round them are grinning faces.

'I've been trying to find you for over an hour,' Captain Black complained. 'You came from under the clouds, while I was 5000 feet up looking for you,' said Mr Williamson, who actually landed after Mary did. But they were all happy, and everyone was given tea. Then the little plane was securely locked away in a shed, to prevent souvenir-hunters from tearing pieces off it. Probably Abe would have liked the key to that shed to have been thrown into the sea. He did not want to have to go through such anxiety ever again. At last he and Mary could collect her battered little suitcases and drive down to Muizenberg, to be together, briefly, in Rust-en-Vrede. Rest and peace. There was need for both.

11

Interlude in South Africa

The flight south, which ended at 12.15 p.m. on 30 April 1928, had taken fifty-two days. The flying hours, Mary calculated, were 121 hours and 35 minutes. These details had to be officially recorded in her logbook. No speed record was broken. But nevertheless the world's press was rapturous.

The *Evening News* in London: 'It is but the bare truth to call Lady Bailey's flight one of the most remarkable accomplishments in aeronautics.'

The *Star*: 'The 8,000 miles were fraught with dangers and close escapes from death.'

Sir Samuel Hoare, the British Secretary of State for Air, sent her a telegram: 'Warm congratulations on successful completion of your flight from London to Cape Town.'

Three days later a luncheon was arranged in Cape Town to honour Abe on the occasion of his retirement from Parliament. It was held in the Mount Nelson Hotel, and was given by both parties of the government. The leaders of the main parliamentary parties were there: General Hertzog, the Prime Minister, and General Smuts, the Leader of the Opposition. The Archbishop of Cape Town and the Chief Justice of South Africa were there. Sir Thomas Smartt, Deputy Leader of the Opposition, presided at the luncheon, with Abe on one side of him and Mary on the other. Sir Thomas said:

Before referring to the reasons which had actuated Sir Abe

Bailey's many friends in having a function of this sort in order to show him the extreme regard in which he is held by his many friends in South Africa, I think we would all, including Sir Abe, agree with me that my first duty is to express, on behalf of all those present, their deep appreciation and pleasure at the happy coincidence of having Lady Bailey also present.

We desire to tender her our sincere felicitations on the wonderful performance which she has accomplished, a performance which has already gained world-wide recognition ... your heroism and daring and enthusiasm have brought you through to our shores from the air. Those of us who know the race from which you have sprung and the Irish blood in you [Sir Thomas was Irish himself], and have the knowledge of your record of heroism and daring in the hunting field, had no doubt that you would come through triumphant ...

Next it was Abe's turn to be praised. Addressing Abe directly, Sir Thomas said:

This gathering is not alone in its regard and affection for you. You are one of those who has made their money in South Africa, but having done so you have not, like so many people who have laid the foundations of their fortune in this country, forgotten the country in which those foundations were laid ... I would like to refer to the gift of the Public Library of South Africa, and the building of the house for the library; the royal subscription which you have given towards the Central Hall of the South African University ...

He went on to talk of the great services Abe had rendered to the agricultural and pastoral development of South Africa.

After this (much longer) eulogy, it was Abe's turn to speak. He started by saying he was reminded, when he entered the room, that he was the inferior person on the occasion.

She has accomplished a noteworthy event in British and South African flying … she has shown all manner of bravery. In the air is her zest for life, and with faith and courage she looks upon death as a very little thing. That is why she is a very daring and skilful airwoman. She almost challenges the unobtainable. I can only protest, as I have done, against that spirit whilst it is still there. But she is as able and ambitious as I am. She has fairly pinned the petticoat to the masthead, and I have no doubt they will allude to me as 'the old woman'. But I will not take this in terms of reproach, but of eulogy. … She was a brave woman when she married me. When I read of her bravery I am almost speechless. I do not know whether to laugh or cry at that bravery, but I could do both. With it all, however, there is an emotion of pleasurable pride excited at times. She would realise anxiety too, if she only knew how I have been bowled at in the ups and downs of life. I have had a good many 'forced landings', and have been 'landed' very often, on the Stock Exchange. Anyone who doesn't believe in luck, good or bad, is entitled to his opinion, but I believe it is through luck that I have been able to warm both hands before the fire of life.

Abe expressed his sadness at leaving parliamentary life. 'My politics now, are how I can help South Africa. I feel that the debt I owe South Africa and South Africans I can never repay.' He went on to say how glad he was to see such excellent feeling existing between the different sections of the House – Dutch and English. He talked of the necessity to bring in more white settlers and secondary industries.

Mary and Abe had only five days together in the Cape. He had long before made plans to sail back to England on the *Arundel Castle* on 5 May. He had tried very hard during those few days to persuade Mary to leave her aeroplane in Young's Field, and to sail home with him by ship. Maybe when he booked his passage he believed he would have no difficulty in persuading her to come with him. But two adamantine wills were in conflict. Hers proved the stronger. When he realized her determination to complete the round trip of her journey by air, she said 'he sportingly did not forbid me to fly back'.

What was to be her excuse to the world this time, for the 8000-mile flight home? The rationale for the southward flight – 'to see my husband' – seemed lame, when their time together turned out to be so short. And most certainly flying home was not the quickest way for her to be reunited with her children, who had already not seen her for two months; going by boat with Abe would have got her back to them in a mere three weeks. It was clear that she was in no hurry at all to return, and she did not, in fact, arrive back in England for another eight months.

Abe was not the only person who attempted to persuade her not to fly back. A Major Miller, the Director of African Airways, was reported in the *Cape Times* on 11 May as 'joining forces with public men who are attempting to dissuade Lady Bailey from returning to England by Airplane'. He said:

> I regret very much that Lady Bailey is flying back. She is taking a great risk of getting fever beside other risks. She will probably be held up in the Sudan, and who is there to escort her? Lady Bailey may not even be able to complete the flight, and I personally wish she would not start. It is no use attempting to minimise the dangers of the solo flight she has just completed. There were two desperate incidents in which fortune favoured Lady Bailey on her journey from Stag Lane to Cape Town. I know Lady Bailey will be angry with me for saying this, but it is only my admiration for her courage and resource that makes me speak.
>
> More regrettable still is the possibility that the non-flying public may regard her return as stunting for a dramatic finish. Those of us who do fly and love the air, know that Lady Bailey has got the flying complex of the air genius. It is the greatest passion of the twentieth century.

This was hitting low, and must have annoyed Mary. But it didn't deflect her. She had adored her lonely odyssey. It had every element that she most relished: risk, speed, adventure, surprise, above all the feeling of overcoming, by herself, great obstacles and hindrances. And closely woven into all this was the feeling of freedom. Who could resist all this? Certainly not Mary, who knew how unfulfilling her life had been before she started flying, and how it had been completely transformed since. And her journey, to her mind, was only half done. In spite of all her apparent modesty, she was infected with the exhilarating fever of competition. Why should she not be the first woman to fly alone both ways? What was there to stop her, after all she had achieved so far, and who was in a better position to do it than she? Her mind was irrevocably set on her return journey by air.

Before she could leave Cape Town, she had several more official functions to attend. A Civic Reception was held in the Cape Town City Hall by the mayor and mayoress. Mary wore 'a charming frock of floral ninon in soft pastel shades on a black ground, and a close fitting "gnome" hat trimmed with feathers'. (This was not what she had worn for the Mount Nelson luncheon – her dress that day had a distinctly rustic look, with smocking across its bodice and a floppy loose-fitting jacket.) Another reception was given for her by the lady members of the Cape Town Flying Club. After that, she made her escape. She was free, she was happy – and incidentally, she was famous.

On Saturday 12 May, Mary went down to Young's Field, hoping to set off for Port Elizabeth, flying east along the Garden Route of the Cape, to avoid the treacherous Hex River mountains. But the weather was against her – a low mist had closed round the airfield. The next day was Sunday, and she decided not to try again until the following day. She finally took off on Monday 14 May. It was not a propitious day for her. Forty-five miles short of Port Elizabeth, the weather got worse and worse, and it grew so dark that she had to find somewhere to land. Just beside Humansdorp she saw what looked like a wide, level road – just right for a forced landing. But its appearance was deceptive, and the hoped-for landing strip turned into a farm lane, with two deep ruts, running either side of a high central ridge, and high banks on both sides of the lane. As she landed the undercarriage hit one of the high banks and collapsed, and the plane tipped forward, crumpling the nose and shattering the propeller, and one wing was slightly damaged. Crestfallen, Mary had to extricate herself and walk to the farm, where the owner, Mike Myers Jr, was able to help her. The plane had to be dismantled and taken to Port Elizabeth by road.

Mary sent a telegram to the staff at Rust-en-Vrede, describing her plight. She then borrowed a plane and pilot from the aerodrome in Port Elizabeth, and flew up to Colesberg, Abe's farmhouse in the Karoo, leaving her damaged plane to be repaired in Port Elizabeth. She stayed in Colesberg for ten days. While she was there she had horses to ride, as Abe's racing stud was there. She had an aeroplane to fly about in, and made various journeys to Kroonstad, and Pietersburg, and to give a talk to the newly formed Aero Club in Bloemfontein. Soon, the redoubtable Major Mentjes came to her rescue again. In the month since her crash in Tabora he had managed to organize the repair of the plane she had crashed there, and when he was told of her latest crash, he flew the newly repaired plane down to her himself at Colesberg, arriving there on Friday 25 May. He stayed there for the weekend, and then flew back with her to Swartkop, the aerodrome at Pretoria, on Monday 27 May.

Mary had now wasted two weeks. What happened next is surprising. Rather than continue her flight in her patched-up Moth, she went to stay with her friend Sir Pierre van Ryneveld and his wife and family, and did not start her flight to London until 21 September – nearly four months later.

What happened to delay her so long is something of a mystery. Certainly she had decided to wait for her second plane to be repaired. Also, she was again having trouble with the British colonial authorities. They were as determined as ever that she should not be allowed to fly alone across southern Sudan. This time there was no one to accompany her. She had therefore to work out a different route for herself. She decided that it would have to be over the west side of Africa – for her, completely unknown territory. She had to find out if there would be landing grounds and supplies of fuel, and what the weather would be like. Sir Pierre's invitation to join him in a big-game hunting expedition might also have had a strong bearing on her decision to stay on with them. Although she had done some shooting with Abe and her stepdaughter Cecil in the early days of her marriage, she had never been big-game hunting, and she couldn't resist it.

She spent most of August and the first part of September in the Maarstrom district of Northern Transvaal, between Pretoria and Bulawayo. 'If anyone wants to feel well and fit, they ought to try this', she wrote later. 'Most of the game saw me before I saw them at first, but later on this got a little better.' And she told a *Rand Daily Mail* reporter that she 'enjoyed every minute of it. Game was plentiful and in great variety, but unfortunately we saw no lions, though we heard them roaring. It was a remarkably fine change, and I enjoyed the camping life.'

She found herself in great sympathy with the farmers of the district, many of whom, she said, were being faced with ruin, because there was an embargo on the shooting of wildebeest, which were overrunning the cattle farms and destroying their grazing. She felt that organized shoots with beaters should be allowed.

If Mary had been a different sort of woman – more like Sophie Heath, perhaps – it would be easy to weave all sorts of romantic possibilities into her long stay with Pierre van Ryneveld and his family. They had so much in common, with his knowledge and love of flying and his record-breaking solo journeys. He was a year younger than Mary – the same age as Tubby Alexander. He had flown in the Great War with the Royal Air Force, and was mentioned in despatches six times, and won the M.C. and the D.S.O. He was, at the time Mary was staying with him in 1928, Director of Air Services in the Union of South Africa. And in that year he obtained a divorce from his wife of seven years, Enid, née Collard, of Croydon. His home was in the Transvaal – at Spikop, near Bronkhorstspruit.

There is no evidence, and no particular reason to suppose, that there was anything more than good friendship between them. (In 1931 Sir Pierre remarried, to Edith Graham, of Warwickshire.) It must have been a joy to Mary to spend time with someone who understood so well why she had to take on these great flights, and who did not discourage her, as Abe did. And he must have helped her to work out what route she would take.

In September Mary was still in the Ryneveld home, and concentrating on the route of her homeward journey. It was hard to discover much practical information about it. Only the Belgian Congo was well documented, with a map for the Belgian Congo Air route. She had two other maps: one from Pretoria to Bulawayo (which she hadn't had on her way down) and a small-scale map of the whole of North-West Africa, as far east as Lake Chad on the north-eastern boundary of Nigeria. The gaps in her maps were prodigious. She had no maps to chart the 2500 miles between Bulawayo and Fort Lamy, near Lake Chad – also, none of Angola or Nigeria. ('But I never knew I was going to visit there!') She was given one for Lake Chad and one for Angola on the way.

She decided she would 'find out from place to place about aerodromes and supplies'. Was it foolhardiness, lack of imagination or impatience with boring practical details that made her so indifferent to the difficulties she might encounter on the way? Certainly she had critics as she started on her homeward journey, who called her both suicidal and foolhardy to be setting forth with so little idea of what might happen to her. But no one could stop her.

By mid-September her second plane – the one she had bought in Nairobi – had had its nose and propeller and wing repaired after the crash-landing in Humansdorp, and was waiting for her at Swartkop aerodrome in Pretoria. She decided to give it a test run from Swartkop to Lourenço Marques (now Maputo), on the east coast of Mozambique – a 250-mile flight. She wrote a long, vivid description of this trial flight to Lourenço Marques and back:

> I was travelling just above the trees (because of low cloud) and then tried going close to the ground where there were no clouds ... being obliged to keep so low in order to distinguish anything at all, I suddenly found a telegraph pole looking as if it wanted to enter the cockpit, so I cleared out of that and continued my route along the railway line.

She spent two nights on this jaunt – one in Ermelo, near Johannesburg, where 'thunderstorms continued all night, and it sounded as if the thunder was being discharged from the veranda outside my bedroom window and it even woke me up', and one in Lourenço Marques – a 'very pretty town in very pretty surroundings'. She flew from there back to Pretoria in 3 hours and 10 minutes, averaging 80 m.p.h. The plane behaved beautifully, and she now felt confident enough to start her marathon journey home.

The actual flight home started from Pretoria, and not, as she had originally planned, from Cape Town. It didn't matter as far as records were concerned: the important thing was that her flight should be from somewhere in South Africa, unaccompanied, back to London.

12

Mary's Flight Journal, Pretoria to Gao

Mary kept a journal during her flight from South Africa to England, making entries intermittently. The entries were not dated, and Mary wrote more than once about certain stretches of flying, sketching them quickly at first and then writing in greater detail when she found herself grounded and with time on her hands. I have supplied the headings, which refer to the day being described rather than the date of composition.

Friday 21 September 1928

I returned to Johannesburg [after her test flight to Lourenço Marques and back on 18 and 19 September], and on the 20th September 1928 I had had a good deal to do and arrange before leaving on the following day, so I packed during the night, and when they came to call me early the next morning, I had not gone to bed or undressed. However, my things were at last weeded down to as small a space as I could well get them, and I went with Dr and Mrs Samuel Evans by car to Pretoria, arriving at Swartkop about 7.0 a.m. There I had to wait until 9.30 until they gave me my log books, before I could leave, and by this time the compass had been swung and corrected. They told me that at 1,000 to 2,000 feet up there was a wind of 30 m.p.h. against me, and that they thought I might not get to Bulawayo. It was getting delivery of the logbooks that was causing me anxiety, and so finally when I got these, I proceeded to take off.

Swartkop is between 5,000 and 6,000 feet altitude above sea level and I had a good load on my little Moth. I taxied busily right across the aerodrome and pulled it off the ground and continued to stay very near the ground heavily for a bit at the start, then was able to climb slowly, and passed over the western side of Pretoria. Somewhere about Warmbaths the wind changed, from northeast to northwest, or so it seemed to me. I travelled over the bush country in the mountains for a while, and then over the same, on a long stretch of flat country, where I could see herds of goodness knows how many wildebeest galloping away from what must have been to them a very faint noise. Herds like these I saw at various intervals, but although I looked for other game, I didn't see any; but the herds of wildebeest must have numbered some hundreds, so perhaps that is why I even noticed them.

I crossed the Limpopo river and steered to the west of my course, and struck a railway line. As I had expected to see Bulawayo town showing somewhere in the distance, and had not realised that the Matopos (mountains there) stretched the length of about 100 miles east to west, I wondered where I had placed myself; however, I turned to the east along the railway line and followed it until I arrived a short while later at Bulawayo, where I landed at 4.10 p.m., having taken 6 hours and 10 minutes on the flight. (Not too bad for wind against.)

They have enlarged the aerodrome at Bulawayo and it is now a completely different proposition to take off and land on it. All around Bulawayo the air seems particularly bumpy, and difficult sometimes for landing on this aerodrome with my vague sort of flying – at least, it is almost necessary to land with the throttle a bit open, as it seems at some seconds difficult to feel a gliding angle at all, even with a very steep glide. Here, by kind invitation and previous arrangements left by Sir John and Lady Chancellor, I lodged at Government House, leaving the following day at 7.10 a.m. to go to Salisbury.

Saturday 22 September
I had no map for this piece of the trip, but after information given, took an angle on the railway line, and a compass course on this. The visibility was not exactly good owing to haze in the air, and I passed over the railway line a shade too west of the direct course,

and eventually (knowing it was not a long trip) got tired of touring into nothingness in haze ahead and seeing nothing, so bore a bit to west and saw very nice country, farms and homesteads. After this, I was much interested in looking at these, and just jobbed about from one lot to another, for the joy of seeing how nice they looked; also, to my west I saw a town or two and a railway line again – this must have been Hartly and some others. Eventually, after wasting a good deal of time but enjoying my sightseeing, I struck a course for Salisbury [Harare], arriving there at 10.30 a.m. Again everyone was most kind, and I enjoyed seeing Salisbury, which I had never visited before.

Sunday 23 September
At 8.00 a.m. I left Salisbury and proceeded along my usual vague compass course taken from striking an angle with the railway – and without a map – to go to Broken Hill. There was a good deal of haze about, which got much thicker later on in the course of this flight. The first mountains I passed over fairly low as I was pretty loaded up. The take-off at Salisbury was all right and the aerodrome good, but there seemed to be a lack of lift in the air surrounding same, and consequently one hung about for a short space, at very little height, above low surrounding trees, before getting any feel that one could climb. Among the trees on top of the first mountains crossed, I saw some big game running from under the trees, scuttling away from the noise of my aeroplane. I refrained from descending lower to see what they were, as I didn't want to have to climb again with my load at the beginning of the trip. They might have been buffalo or hartebeests, or some big buck – I don't even know what exists in those mountains. After a while I got into mountainous country: here there were many veldt fires, and the haze got thicker and thicker; at last I could see peaks a bit too high for me in patches in the haze, and then could barely see even below me. So, as soon as I sighted yellow streaks of sand, denoting a river bed, I followed same to west, in order to try and get clear of some of the high ground, and to avoid having an unseen mountainside in front of my machine. The haze got a shade better, and the mountains a shade less high, so I left the river bed and turned

[113]

on to my self-made compass course again. Here, before long, I got into the same deadlock with more haze and more high mountains, so I took another sand river-bed as soon as I crossed one, and bore west. Following this again, the ground got a bit lower and the haze less, so that I could see a little, and I crossed over the Kafue river. I was rejoicing heartily at seeing this river, as I knew that this and the railway further on were my only two known landmarks: however, when I saw below me through a haze a stretch of what looked like grey-green water, dotted with what seemed like muddy or sandy stretches of banks, both in the river as islands and along the bank, without vegetation and without apparently a living thing, I thought it was not such a pleasant sight after all. Then more mountains, and more haze, and then eventually the land became lower and less hazy and I saw a road or two, finally bits of cultivation, which showed I had got back to the land of the living once again. Next I saw the railway, and after a still somewhat hazy but pleasant trip of about three-quarters of an hour, following this northwards I arrived at Broken Hill at 12.30 p.m.

Here at Broken Hill I met some friends, and obtained petrol and oil, and left at 2.05 on the same day, to go to Elizabethville. The take-off with a load in the middle of the hottest part of the day at Broken Hill was not an easy task; the wind was blowing the smoke from the chimney-stacks near the aerodrome, first in one direction, and then a second or two later in the opposite one – so there was not going to be any help from that source. The first time I tried to get off I could see that I would never be able to see, as there were some trees at the far end of the aerodrome, so I throttled down and taxied back to the starting point.

Next time I ran at it all I could, and then pulled off the ground; had no pull, so was obliged to pull up over a tree, then put the machine on side to avoid one on each side that I could not get over. I expected the Moth to give in and start dropping at any moment, but luckily the trees further on were somewhat sparse, so I was able to stick the nose of the Moth well down, and steer in and out through the trees, near the ground, to keep going. After that all was well, but it was quite an exciting take-off for me while it lasted, and I had my head bobbing out first on one side and then the other, trying to see where there was a tree to avoid, and hoping I had not got one right in front of me hidden by the engine – in fact, I was 'very busy flying' during those seconds!

As I did not think I had enough daylight to allow me to follow the railway line round N'Dola, I again took an angle with the railway line, and took a compass course on that, to hit off Elizabethville, as I hadn't got a map for this piece either. After once more finding haze and a good deal of marshy country and numerous small rivers, and having flown for some time, I knew I ought to have struck the railway, but as I had not seen a sight of it, and as at Elizabethville, or even just south of this, the railway line turns north, I imagined I must have got too much to the west, with drift from a south-east wind, which was blowing. I crossed two big roads, which I went down low over and looked at most anxiously, trying to invent an imaginary pair of railway lines along them, but they were only wheeltracks! I struck a bit of 'east' into my course, and proceeded onwards. So far, my whole course from Broken Hill had covered country of marsh and swamp and river, where it would have been impossible to land a machine – easy to clear, to make landing grounds, but otherwise not possible. I struck a railway line and felt as joyful as seeing the Kafue river at first in the morning's flight. It was a very distinct, clear new railway line – large as life – and in a moment or two of my following it, it ended: I thought it must have gone into a tunnel but it had not! It was a mine, and no-one seemed to have a landing ground there, or appeared at all interested in seeing a Moth veering erratically around the terminus of their railway line. Well, with great disappointment I left that end of their railway line and proceeded to go along in the opposite direction, thinking that that must lead to the main line, and also deciding that aerodrome or no aerodrome, the first town I came to I must land at, because the sun was so low already. I came to the main line and turned *south* along it, then to a few houses and dwellings and sheds, and as bad a possible piece of ground that one could have landed on but not taken off from; noting this in my mind, I continued to follow the railway line southwards, and suddenly, round a large curve, came upon a town of fair size, with wireless masts, so I decided that whatever place it was, I was landing there somewhere before dark. There appeared to be no aerodrome near the surrounding mines and mine dwellings, so I then began looking for a bit of ground where I might land, and yet be able to take off from. It was not easy to pick. Finally, I went to look at one I had seen in the distance, and blessed if there was not a most suitable long strip of cleared land *and a hangar* as well!! In great glee I landed on it, and was going to ask what place it was, when I saw Mr. Murdoch (who I knew was at Elizabethville with his Avion, that he had done his record flight from England to the Cape on), so I did not even have to ask what town it was.

Having said that I had no map to fly on from Bulawayo to Salisbury, and from Salisbury to Broken Hill, and from there to Elizabethville, I mean I had no map to take a course off. I had two pages of the Union Castle Co's map book showing half the course to Salisbury, but as this measured, with the margins and all, a total of about 5 inches long by about 3 inches wide, and showed an enormous amount of another part of the continent of Africa, also condensed into the same page, and only half way on the route I wanted, it did not show me much, but what it did show me was all I had to go on. On the other hand, as long as one managed eventually to arrive somewhere it certainly saved a lot of trouble. But one had not the slightest idea as to whether the degrees one had noticed the compass to be showing at the moment one had chosen an angle on the railway line at the start were going to be correct, because they were a guess, as I did not even have the whole of the route (only to half-way) on the small page out of the Union Castle book. To anyone who knows the country it may be all right, but to anyone like myself, who had never been over it before, it was an 'unknown quantity'. Still, it worked all right.

I arrived at Elizabethville at 5.15 on the 23rd September, and stayed there three days.

Wednesday 26 September

On the 26th September I left Elizabethville at 7.30 a.m. It was bush country in the mountains till Bukama; N'Gule was very pretty country: big pasture plains and mountains to the N.E. and a few farms. I followed the inside curve of the Sabena route, with its strips of cleared ground as emergency landing grounds, and with their map marked out and very little haze, I felt I was travelling in state. I landed at Kamina at 11.15 and got petrol, and could find no mineral oil that I could use, so took Sabena Co's mineral oil 'Vedol', which I knew I did not like the look of. However, there was nothing else to be done. The country from Bukama to Kamina was grassland with some bush land at the beginning in patches. I left Kamina at 1.0 and after passing level with Luluabourg [now Kananga] (which town one could not see from the regular route) I noticed my oil gauge descending; I knew I had probably only one hour 20 minutes or so to go on, to get to Musese [Luebo] Aerodrome, so shook the Moth up a bit and glided down to empty the auxiliary oil tank into the sump. The gauge went up again for a moment or two, and then began to drop again. I tried the same trick with the same result, so went back to the emergency landing ground at Tehumba, near a Mission (and level with Luluabourg on map) and landed with great care, having first circled around the mission. Then hundreds upon hundreds of blacks ran and arrived panting and much heated – men, women and children of all ages, all talking, yelling, and much interested and excited. Finally, after a bit I found one among them who was dressed in a shirt and a hat, who spoke French, and he said they would come later with a motor from somewhere, so I asked that the crowd, which continued to grow, and which were all yelling at once continuously, should move further back and keep a space between their circle and the aeroplane. The pandemonium raged while with more yelling and waving of sticks they moved back, only to be pushed forward again by those behind! And so it went on for ages – the grass had been long on the land ground, and my wings cut this as I landed, just like a patent mowing machine, I did most of my landing before touching ground, and switched off directly on touching ground, so only ran about 15 or 20 yards, if as much. After a while some white people arrived there: some of the Fathers from the Mission. They all had a try at forcing the blacks back, to leave a bigger circle, but with the same results as before, and the noise never ceased. After two hours, when the sun had set, the Administrator arrived with some guards to guard the machine. Then I got them to fill sacks with earth, and we tied it down, covered it up, and in the darkness left to walk to the road and get a car.

Thursday 27 September
I stayed the night there [Tehumba] and next morning early there was a dense *white* fog over everything – this lifted partly, about 9 o'clock, so that one could see to walk on foot. It left the grasses and plants as if hung with hoar frost, and some time later on when the sun first got through, it was a veritable fairyland picture. I saw pineapples growing for the first time, and various other plants. They had to cut the grass on the landing ground before I could leave, and I was given a 6 gallon tin of Mobiloil by M. Dumont, who would accept no payment. I imagine it would be a heavy oil to use for a 'Cirrus' engine in Europe, but in the heat it seems to answer grand.

I left Tehumba at 11.30, and arrived at Musese aerodrome at 12.25. The railway line having disappeared into the forests completely, or rather the road, as it was no longer a railway line to follow, after Kalenda, or a bit west of that, the forests were so thick with giant trees and the tops of these so close that you could not see any branches even. I flew up high to get a glimpse of a road anywhere, passing through any clearing ahead, as I did not wish to miss locating the aerodrome of Musese, which should be somewhere near. This worked all right. [She landed at Musese.] There were thunderstorms all night, and next morning low clouds over forests all around, except clearer to eastwards, which was the way I had come and no use to me!

Friday 28 September
I started at about 11 o'clock; tried to keep below clouds low down on tops of trees, but the clouds were all round in patches and to the ground, so I went above and looked through the holes. Then I met a big curtain of higher cloud, too high to go over, and quite dense inside, and no space between that and the lower lot, so I tried to get back to the aerodrome and find it by looking through the holes in the clouds. There, below one hole, only dense forest – another hole, only dense forest, and so on. So at last I took out my map and

looked at that and the compass, and decided which way I had come out, and where I must strike, and I hit off the aerodrome all right. Once there, it was a bit clearer, so I tried north and south to see if there was an opening, but no good. So I landed eventually, and left, with still very low clouds, at 12.10. This time, however, I had a chance by keeping very low, and kept along over tops of trees going around to keep in dips and hollows and creeks, to keep under the clouds. I got the big river Kasai, and followed this, low over it, till Eolo. Then the sky cleared and I went up to 4,000 feet, and arrived at Bandundu at 4 o'clock. (Asked why I flew so high – I said because it was a change to creeping along the tops of the trees.)

Mary added detail to her account of the journey between Elizabethville and Léopoldville, probably while grounded with engine trouble for seventeen days in Luanda, Angola, or while in Léopoldville for nearly a month recovering from abscesses on her legs and feet.

Elizabethville is a big town for the Congo, and surrounded by mines and mine dwellings. Much is being done in the town since the recent visit of the King and Queen of the Belgians, to lay out streets, to clean and tidy up those in existence, and the buildings and shops. Flowering trees grow in an avenue edging the sides of most of the main streets; there is a good deal of dust and it is fairly hot. There are two or three hotels and plenty of shops, many of them kept by South Africans or English, or those foreigners who have lived for some time in South Africa. The surrounding country is bush, with huge anthills everywhere, about 30 feet high. Somewhere among these, near the town there is a golf course.

Kamina was merely a railway station with railway workshops and a few dwellings for those officials belonging to the railway.

Luluabourg I did not see, as it is off the present air route on the river of this name, and a bit too north of the Sabena route, and is, I believe, a town. I was told they had a good aerodrome there, and that it is where the air route will eventually pass, but their aerodrome is not marked on their map.

After this, before long the forest region commences and the roads etc. cease, and you come to the Kasai River – a very big one with a strong current and many shifting sandbanks in it. The river boats and steamers are the means of transport for commerce, for administration and everything. The rest, either side, as far as one looks, is forest – palm trees and trees of many kinds, but no firs or pines etc., and they say none of these grow anywhere in the Belgian Congo. Bananas, pineapples, bread trees, mango trees and pau pau grow wild – or like weeds when planted. Some of the bananas in some parts are copper-coloured and softer and more juicy to eat. Some of the ordinary sort grow to a foot at least in length, in huge branches.

There are wireless stations at Elizabethville, Port Francki and Kinshasa, and also at Brazzaville on the north side of the Congo River, opposite to Kinshasa, and the French town in the French Congo. Brazza, the French explorer, according to account, travelled on foot through (it must have been more like cutting, forcing and struggling through) these vast lands and forests, at the same time as Stanley was doing the same thing for the Belgians, I think they said it was about 50 years ago.

Bandundu at present is only a port for commerce, with one private residence belonging to the administrative head of that region, and there are warehouses and loading and unloading of cargo on and off the river boats. Bandundu is at the junction of the Kwanza [Kwango] and Kasai rivers. The Kwanza has the fastest running deep volume of water I have ever seen, except perhaps the river Congo at Boma. The Kwanza river starts in Angola somewhere, and no small boat of any description could ever live in that current running past Bandundu. These big rivers abound in crocodiles, and the forest – they say – in elephants etc., snakes and insects in plenty. A caterpillar or centipede that was given to me to take back for verification as to what species it belonged to, at Musese – it was about 1 inch broad, and about 4½ to 5 inches long; light green, with masses of legs, and a tail shaped like that of an earwig (roughly); and if it touched a person gave them the most awful fever (so the story went), that simply took violent effect straight away, and crippled them or killed them. This one had been caught by petrol being poured over it, and a match set to it, so its feet are burnt, but these were cream or white in colour.

After Eolo on the Kasai River the dense forest ends, but though

Mary after getting her pilot's licence (left), and in turban after head injury, 1927

At Brooklands, 1927

At Stag Lane before the flight to South Africa, with (clockwise from upper left) Ann, Noreen, Jim and Derrick, January 1928

Being greeted by Abe after landing in Cape Town, 30 April 1928; the photo was cropped in Mary's album

At the Mount Nelson Hotel, Cape Town, on the occasion of a luncheon honouring Abe. Prime Minister Hertzog is between Abe and Mary, and Jan Smuts is to Mary's right

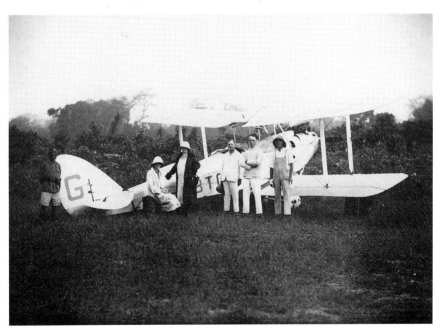

Fogbound in Coquilhatville, 16 November 1928

Landing at Croydon at the end of the South Africa–England flight, 17 January 1929

At Croydon with Mary Ellen, Noreen and her brother Willie

Cartoon from Punch, *30 January 1929*

On the Kharga Oasis expedition, 1929

Above: *Four famous aviatrixes, Mary, Amelia
    Earhart, Amy Johnson and Winifred Spooner, 1932*
Right: *Mary as a WAAF officer, 1941*
Below: *Abe and Mary on their way to a Buckingham
    Palace garden party, early 1930s*

Above: *Presentation at court, 1937*
Left: *With nephew Paddy, 1938*
Below: *With daughters Ann and Noreen at Cape Town airport, c. 1948*

With gamekeeper Paddy McGuinness at Rossmore (left), and outside The Mains, Kenilworth, Cape Town, shortly before her death

The burial place of Abe and Mary, on the cliff above Rust-en-Vrede

there are large grass plains, there are as yet no roads, and all transport and means of communication is by way of the river boats. The Congo River is big, comes down from the north and flows south, broadening into Stanley Pool, with a large island in the centre. This is like a *very large* lake, and ends at the south-west in the town of Leopoldville on the southern bank [Belgian] and Brazzaville on the northern bank [French].

The natives, between Eolo and Leopoldville, seemed a slight race – either small or else a fairly weedy looking lot: a few were a bit more robust looking. I was told they suffered much from illness, as they would not cease taking concoctions of herbs etc., made by themselves, which acted as drugs, and that when they were ill it was difficult to get them to go and see a white doctor. There was a good deal of sleeping sickness in those forests. The natives all through the forest parts of the Congo are said to be great runners, and will take a message on foot for unthought-of distances, if sent on a mission, in a comparatively short while. They also have their own particular mode of wireless telegraphy – the drums with their own type of Morse code to use for this.

Saturday 29 September – Thursday 18 October
I left Bandundu next morning at 10 o'clock, arriving at Kinshasa, Leopoldville, at 12.30.

On the evening of my arrival at Leopoldville I flew across the river to Brazzaville and landed, to ask the Governor there for information and help about petrol and oil etc., for my journey through French territory, after I left Coquilhatville. He was very kind, but not very informative – very kindly gave me a map (which I had not got of that region) and said he was quite sure I should get supplies as far as Fort Lamy; but after that he said he could tell me nothing. He said there was a wireless at Fort Lamy to replace telegraphy, as the giraffes had continually ran into and broke the telegraph line between there and Zinder etc.

Well on Monday 1st October, while waiting the arrival of replies to some cables sent to England, I thought I would like to see Boma and Angola, so flew that day from Kinshasa to Boma. Landed there to get petrol and oil to continue journey, but found no B.B. oil, and the town was 17 km from the aerodrome, so I had to get my oil and stay the night. The aerodrome at Boma is not enormous, and has a hill suddenly in the middle of it, and is surrounded by a big open drain, so that one has to come in alongside the hangar and land just on it, and run to the middle and no more. I had left Leopoldville at 9.20 a.m. and arrived at Boma at 12.25.

On Tuesday 2nd October I left Boma at 7.45 a.m. and arrived at Loanda [Luanda] at 10.55.

There was a lot of low cloud, and I could not get near the sea coast, and muddled along in and out of clouds, flying as low as ever I could. I had to go through some of it, as there was no avoiding it, but kept due south on a compass course for due south, because clouds seemed a shade better on the eastern side. When these got a bit better, I put some 'west' into my course, and eventually saw the sea in the distance. About three-quarters of an hour before reaching Loanda – when the clouds got better – I saw a whole lot of game not far from one of the rivers I went down, and chased these about for a bit. They were, I should have said, rhinoceros, as their heads were so long, but the gentry of Loanda swore they must be hippopotamuses. Anyhow they were mighty stocky animals, and I got them galloping about fine, which was very funny, as they did not look as if they would have been able to gallop. There were two fair-sized herds of them which eventually joined up; further on I saw some buffaloes and then some fairly large buck – they must have been roan-antelope, but I could not distinguish their horns, as it was a bad day for seeing, and still very misty.

Loanda was an old town of stucco and plaster houses painted in various colours; the sea in front, and the sandy beach, and the long narrow strip of island, and the red sandy cliff behind, and then high plateau land above. This was obviously a bit of the 'ancient', after all the new houses and warehouses of the Belgian Congo. The people were Portuguese – there were a lot of mulattoes. There was no regular 'native quarter' or 'village' to the town – they seemed to be allowed to live about anywhere. The town was very pretty, both from the air and from the ground, and as at Lourenço Marques, the Portuguese explorers seemed to know how to choose their sites for founding a town most admirably. I landed, and on

trying my switches, found that the front magneto wasn't functioning. They had masses of motor cars in Loanda, and every one of
them seemed to be at the aerodrome, and crowds of excited
people. They had had a strike of police or something, and the
guards for the aeroplanes had been asked for, but evidently didn't
intend to put in an appearance, so we waited there for them for
about 1½ hours, till at last, after much suggestion on my part,
someone did finally take a car and go and get them. When they
arrived I took a photograph of them, and they seemed pleased as
punch about this.

Well, the front magneto was not easy to get restarted: it was
giving a spark on each plug, and it seemed functioning all right, but
was firing on wrong stroke on wrong cylinder. I would not let
anyone take both magnetos off and re-time my engine, as one
mechanic after another wished to do. And then, finally, I took a
front magneto off and found the spring of the impulse starter was
broken in two places. Well, then I knew the spring was not likely
to have been a weak one, nor did it look it, but I could not think
what could have caused it to break; also, I could not get to the
rights of how the whole thing worked, as the result of an odd sort
of coupling arrangement between that and the spring and the front
magneto.

The following day, Wednesday 3rd October, the Portuguese
flight of two Vickers machines with two pilots, an observer and a
mechanic, who had flown from Lisbon and were on their way to
Lourenço Marques, arrived and landed at Loanda. Their mechanic
very kindly had a look at my trouble, but could not decipher the
cause either. The amount of times I checked over that front magneto with different mechanics was tremendous. We found another
piece of metal cracked on the impulse starter, putting it out of
shape, and that was another clue.

The Portuguese aviators stayed and were fêted in Loanda for
about three or four days, and then departed on their way – then I
went at my puzzle, while the workshops in the town meanwhile
copied me the cracked piece of metal and turned the spring afresh.
They could not renew this, so it had to be used shorter. At last, I
found that all depended on a small flat metal washer with a key

way that had been hardly dealt with at some time, and had worn, allowing the face on which the spring and the mechanism of its tightening and releasing to slip to a different position. Naturally the spring did not get released, it went on tightening up, and had to break, and the timing of the front magneto got all wrong in consequence of this too. So then I got a new washer made, and a spare one, and all was well.

Meanwhile, I was taken out shooting in the vicinity at night in a car with a spotlight, by some of the kind and hospitable dwellers of Loanda who had befriended me. It was great fun: we did not see much during the night – got a small buck – missed a roan antelope, and when daylight came sighted a herd of buffaloes, which we stalked first in the car across the veldt, and then on foot – we got three, and then returned to the town.

Finally, I had my new piece safely replaced in my engine, and did my best to get them all fixed correctly; also the timing of the front magneto, and then I started off for Boma.

Friday 19 October

I left Loanda at 1 o'clock and arrived at Boma at 4 o'clock. The same fogs were all over the coast, right down on to the water, so I just struck inland, due east alongside of the low cloud, till I saw a passageway eventually between the low clouds to the north, and turned up this. Keeping my eyes on these gaps of clear, I flew on northwards through one or another place; then it got better, and on arriving at the river it was not so good visibility again. I landed and stayed the night.

Saturday 20 October – Friday 9 November

I went on to Leopoldville, leaving Boma at 11.30 and arriving in Leopoldville at 2 o'clock. Here, as I was in the act of leaving for Bandundu and Coquilhatville, I was stopped by kind friends and advised to wait for medical attention to some abscesses which I had got on my legs and feet, as a result of scratching mosquito bites, and which were already causing me a good deal of trouble. I was glad later of the advice, as they were very painful, though nothing otherwise to worry about. I was not allowed to walk about, and had bandages galore, no stockings, bedroom slippers, and as it was very hot and one was sticky (to say the least of it!) all day, I was in need of clothes. Ready-made ones were not to be had, and I had had to imagine myself a dressmaker already in Loanda, for the same reasons, and make two frocks; so I made some more at Leopoldville, and must have looked a prettier sight than ever.

Saturday 10 November
I flew over to Brazzaville, to see Monsieur Bulmer. I had heard that a French flight with Lieutenant Marie and Lieutenant Bulmer and a mechanic, which had left Paris on a 'Breguet' (can't spell. M.B.); crossed to Oran, crossed the Sahara from Reggan to Gao and flown via Archambault, Bangui, Coquilhatville, Bandundu, to land on the same landing ground near Luluabourg as I had landed, on coming from the other direction; Tehumba, near the Mission, and that on landing they had got one wheel into a soft piece of ground and turned their machine, an all-metal one, over – crumpling up the longerons etc. beyond repair, but without damage to themselves. They had reached there in nine days from Paris, and were trying to get to Madagascar in 12 days, which they thought they surely would have done if they had not had this bad luck. I flew over to Brazzaville to see M. Bulmer, and to get what information I could.

He said that the Sahara would be hopeless in case of a forced landing, but that so long as I went on a compass course and did not try to follow tracks of the motor cars which cross there, he thought I could not lose my way but that without a wireless apparatus on my machine it would be hopeless to expect to be found if I had to make a forced landing. He was waiting at Brazzaville to get information from Paris as to what they should do.

Friday 16 – Saturday 17 November
As soon as I was allowed, I got off and flew to Bandundu. In the agitation of packing and of saying goodbye, etc. etc., I did not fasten the buckle of my sun-helmet carefully enough, and so after I'd been going about ten minutes flight from Leopoldville up the river towards Bandundu, I felt a tug, and looked round just in time to see my helmet flying away past the tail of my machine into

space over the river. Luckily there were lots of clouds about. The only thing I could lay my hands on was a flour bag that some maps were in beside me in the machine, so I emptied these out and shoved the flour bag under my leather flying helmet, to raise it. No harm was done, and someone gave me an old sun-helmet of theirs at Bandundu, for which I was most grateful, and which, not being meant for a flying helmet, played a sort of ping-pong and see-saw on my head all the while.

Having left Leopoldville at 9.15 I arrived at Bandundu at 11.15; got petrol, and awaited the arrival of the Sabena Co's aeroplane, which was due to call there that same day, en route from Coquilhatville to Leopoldville, with M. Orta on board, as he had been most kind, and given every help with advice, information and mechanical assistance at Leopoldville, and I wanted to thank him. They had made me two spare springs out of the tops of saws in the workshop at Leopoldville, to take with me in case the one on my Moth – broken and rendered so much shorter at Loanda – should at any time not bear the extra tension put on it, and give out.

The Sabena Company run their air route from Elizabethville to Boma – a fortnightly service, with big passenger three-engine Handley Page machines, having two Siddeley-Puma engines and one Rolls Royce engine each, and carrying about (as far as I can remember) twelve to sixteen passengers, together with freight and luggage. They have been using this air service on this route now for three years, and have run it with 100% efficiency. The machines leave regularly to time, and arrive regularly to time also, and considering the varied nature of the country flown over, and the tornadoes to be found in those parts – to say nothing of fog and low clouds – it is a pretty good all-round performance. M. Orta has been the originator and organiser of the route, and planned all the organisation, which seems admirably carried out by those belonging to the company in the various capacities under his direction. They run branch routes from the main one, and, I believe, intend to extend this to other parts, and are ready to take on the making of a route from any terminus of their present route to anywhere, as far as I could judge. They laid out the landing ground at Brazzaville, and laid out emergency landing grounds along the coast to Loanda, and have resurrected the wartime aerodrome at Loanda. Most of their aerodromes and the emergency landing grounds are long narrow strips facing into the direction of the prevailing wind, and marked with a large white circle. At the regular aerodromes there are large hangars, and at some there are rest houses for the passengers to lodge at. The mechanic who looks after each machine, travels on that machine, and the government, after giving the Company a guarantee of so much per annum, per machines in regular use, pay their subsidy according to the amount of weight in freight and passengers carried by the company. The pilots, so far as I could hear of their records, were all pretty well-picked men, who had had experience and outstanding performances to their credit in Belgium. This route goes at present also from Bandundu to Coquilhatville, and will soon be in working order to Bangui; while the French are to extend their Toulouse – Malaga – Gao – Niamey – Zinder – Fort Lamy – Fort Archambault and Bangui route, and so link this up as well, and by the same year the French say they will inaugurate a service from Paris by either of these two routes to Dakar, that will go from Dakar across to South America – as they say that crossing the Atlantic by the southern seas means mainly fair weather, whereas in the north the weather over the Atlantic is mainly atrocious.

Well, to return to my journey: the big passenger 'plane arrived at Bandundu, and M. Orta said I must be off at once, because as soon as the morning was past you got very bad tornadoes on the trip to Coquilhatville, and especially around Lac Leopold II. So off I set, and sure enough, I saw a fat tornado before I ever got to Lac Leopold II, and steered a course to the side, so as to avoid it, but after a while I saw it would catch me, and that there was a good deal of lightning going on in the middle of the storm, so I just turned tail and fled in the opposite direction, till cleared of such close proximity; then went on watching clouds and sky ahead, to keep in the clear, and keep under patches of blue sky. The tornadoes were truly collecting round this large lake, and would soon join in one closed-in mass over it. I thought that whenever I had made an attempt to paint a picture that would not be recognisable as to colour or form, I could always splodge it a bit and write underneath 'A Tornado'. You could see every conceivable colour in these clouds.

After Lac Leopold II I was still veering about, to east–west of my course from the east side to Lac Tumba. I then crossed this lake, and proceeded on a compass course into space over the forests: from the beginning of Lac Leopold II, all that was not lake was forest. Huge trees, and masses upon masses – all dark below, except where a gap would show the glint of the sun on water – they were all growing and standing in water, and it is said that the resin and sap from the trees, oozing into this water, forms the copal, that the Belgians trade in greatly. All this same forest stretched all the way to the Congo river again, and all around Coquilhatville, forest and marsh, marsh and water everywhere. Coquilhatville [now Mbaandaka] was the most wonderful spot for vegetation – damp and steamy, and absolutely beautiful to look at. It is actually on the equator, and seems to grow every kind of tree, shrub, plant and flower; but most of these things I had never seen or heard of before. The town is served for transport, for communication and for trade, by the river. Five rivers actually have their junction here, with the Congo. Everything is dense: the blackness under the trees; the profusion of these, and plants and bamboos and reed and creeping plants. They have the most wonderful Botanical Garden here – Eyala – the fourth best and most important of the world, I was told. I had never heard of it, but stayed over a day to see it.

The aerodrome was a cleared strip of forest with bushes etc. growing all over it except for a built roadway running north and south on the eastern edge. As the whole thing is marsh, one lands, takes off and taxis on this bit of roadway alone. It is the Sabena Co's latest addition to their air route, and they are building a hangar there. Northwards of Coquilhatville there are as yet no prepared emergency landing grounds any more, but these have already been picked, and work is proceeding at some of these at the present time, to prepare them.

Sunday 18 November
I left Coquilhatville at 9.0 a.m., and arrived at Bangui at 1.30. Forest, dense forest again, first in marshes, then, just at the finish,

forest growing on dry ground and near Bangui, roads from Ubangi (Belgian side) and one on French side, and the Ubangi river gives a big curve to the east, and goes over some rapids; the flat country becomes hilly, with small trees; and at the foot of these little green tree-clad hills, and by the river at the rapids, the town of Bangui – the last navigable calling-place of the river boats from Brazzaville (as, owing to the rapids, they can go no further). Here the aerodrome was square, as hard as a rock and somewhat bumpy of surface, but otherwise a very good one.

Bangui was the first place north of the equator where I found horses, as, owing to the flies and mosquito, etc., there had not been any kept in the towns of the Belgian Congo which I had visited. Even at Elizabethville they said that horses did not live long if imported there. I had to stay over the next day at Bangui, as during the night and that day there were continual tornadoes: the sky, hills and surrounding country, the river and even the buildings next door to the house where I was staying were blotted out from view, and torrents of rain fell in spasms all the time.

Tuesday 20 November

I took off at 10.10 when a fog – the result of the rains of the day before – had cleared up and the clouds lifted enough, and took a compass course for Fort Archambault [Sarh]. I was told there were two good roads; one going more to the east and the other more to the west, which led to Fort Archambault; but I kept a course between these. The western road showed up at about half way, on my west, for a short while, and then went to the west again; it was a grand big road and showed up well. The country was hilly, with small trees all the first part of the way, and then the country goes flat, with rivers and river beds, and sort of short scrub on the second part of my way. I arrived at the river Shari and at Fort Archambault, where I found an excellent aerodrome: here I was received by the Administrator and a crowd of natives, and a native band which started playing for all they were worth the second I shut off my engine, and continued to do so. It was pretty hot on the ground – I arrived at 3 o'clock – and after the usual procedure of posting guards around the Moth, filling three sacks full of earth and tying

the machine down with these; covering up the propeller, the cock-
pits and pulling out all my various small sacks constituting my luggage, the latter were given to some porters who carried them
balanced on their heads. Then the Administrator got into one special kind of rickshaw – a cross between that and a bath chair with
shafts – and I got into another, with the band still playing away
hard, and we proceeded at a slow walking pace through the main
street of the native town. The band consisted mainly of drums of
various sizes and lengths, beaten with the hands, accompanied by
some instruments looking and sounding exactly like the bagpipes
but without the bag, and also by what looked like a very long coach
horn with pieces of rags and stuffs binding it up for most of its long
length – it emitted an intermittent sound every few seconds into
the general mêlée of music, and sounded rather like a large cow
whose calf had just been taken away from her. The walking pace
we went was not a very fast one, and at this speed we took quite a
little time to cover the distance of the main street of the native village before we arrived at the Administrator's house. As the whole
native population had turned out – men, women and children all
accompanying us on either side and behind – some dancing to the
music and running in front, one had ample opportunity to study
their general appearance. They were black and huge in the way of
height – six to seven feet must have been the average of men and
women, and what surprised me so much was that they were not
only perfectly proportioned for their height, but were an all round
average of the best built race that I have ever seen. Their faces
looked open, frank and broad, and I must say, that I have not seen
a race like this one since. (I am writing this at Gao during an
enforced wait here.) It appears this is one particular race peculiar
to this part.

The band stayed to play for some time outside the residence of
the Administrator and his wife, while we sat and tried to talk to one
another on the verandah. After a while the band ceased, peacefully,
and had a well-earned rest, and we also!

That evening I was offered a bath, and as it was after dark, and
the mosquitoes reigned in millions, I wondered if getting the bath
was worth while for as soon as I undressed I was attacked all over

the whole time; however, I got through with the bath and returned to the company at their dinner party, scratching as many parts as I could well manage at the same time!

Wednesday 21 – Thursday 22 November
Petrol and oil was sent for early, and carried up to the aerodrome, and I was taken up riding pillion on a motor bike – the only conveyance or motor in the place: everyone journeyed on horseback or foot in those parts – and I proceeded with the usual round of cleaning and clearances etc. on my Moth. At 10.30 I took off, and arrived at Fort Lamy [now N'djamena] at 2.30. I took a compass course, and the country seemed flat everywhere; there seemed to be a bit of a haze, and one could not see long distances clearly. One gradually got over what looked like bare, barren scrub, with marshes and lines denoting small rivers and river beds. Later on there were a good many large veldt fires, but the last piece on the way towards Fort Lamy was pretty well populated with native villages, etc.

At Fort Lamy the aerodrome was V-shaped, and had an excellent surface; you could have likened it to a billiard table. This town was again on the Shari river. This aerodrome – the whole country being cotton soil – in the rainy season becomes flooded or soft mud, so I was told. But they are to build a permanent raised road as a runway on which to land and take off in the wet season. I stayed one day at Fort Lamy, and had a real peaceful clean-up at my Moth.

Friday 23 – Saturday 24 November
I took off at 7.55 a.m., by way of going to land for petrol and oil at Maidugari and from there on to Kano – both in Nigeria. I passed over Maidugari and had a good look at it: there seemed to be no landing ground, and certainly none marked. I was travelling with the tail edge of the French map given me at Brazzaville: this showed nothing on it as soon as it was over the French border, except three dots marked Dikoa, Maidugari and Kano, on a white and otherwise blank ground. I had been told there was a road to follow all the way, but although I picked this up after crossing the

river at Fort Lamy, I missed it soon after, as a result of admiring the scenery, which was still all flat country. I saw a lot of small lines to the south-west, denoting small rivers, so I went north-west to pick up the road, and when I found a road I followed this, but it went southwards soon afterwards for so long that I wondered if it was the right one. I could see that ahead and to the south of me there was a highish band of white fog in the distance, and after a while, sticking up in the distance, over the top of this to the south, and then to the south-east, I saw the black and dark tops of mountains. These I was told later must have been the mountains of the Cameroons.

Below, the white band of fog hid out all distance – the town I could see I took to be Dikoa [now Dikwa] because of no circle denoting an aerodrome. In reality, however, it must have been Maidugari, and going for the first time eastwards as I was doing, I had a following wind, so was doing much quicker time than had been the case on any previous journeys. Shortly, I got into the band of white fog, which then turned brown, and was what they called Hamataan – a wind raising a fog of sand and dust all over the country. I could see below me, and as I was following a road, I just kept on, but had to fly low: the wind must have been fairly strong and it was a shade bumpy.

After going for three hours, I knew I must have got beyond Maidugari, and that the road having gone so much south, I might be making for Jos instead of Kano, and as the visibility by this time was bad, I landed down in a native village, where the main street seemed fairly wide and good. I had a good look at it first, and saw that there were telegraph posts on one side, close on to the motor road, but on the other side was a sandy track for the camels, etc., with room for my wings that side, between that and the mud huts lining the streets.

My first perusal of this brought the whole populace into the main street, and I wondered if they would understand that I wished to land; so, to try this out, I pretended that I was about to do so, and waved them to clear away. This they seemed to understand at once, and cleared straight off. Then I came round again, and steered as best and carefully as I could, as I had to remember to keep to the side track, which was a different level to the road;

and about telegraph wires on the other side; and I could see I would have to get down over two trees and between some others, and run along the ground under some others. This sounds as if there were many difficulties, but it was not so – only a few obstacles there were, which needed watching, for my kind of flying.

I landed, and managed to keep straight, and then saw that at the last moment some old women and very young children had rushed out of the houses on either side, ahead of me into the street, but I knew I dared pay no attention to them, as I had to hold my run-in dead straight, so hoped they would run fast enough away again ... out of the corner of my eye I could see black forms legging it as if they were winning a race, on either side in front, and disappearing into the houses again like rabbits down their holes with a terrier after them; and followed with tremendous scuttling by the small, black, fat children.

The crowd then came around again, and I found one among them who spoke a little English. He said, so far as I could understand, that that was the road to Kano; that I had passed Maidugari, and that Mr King, who owned a car, would 'give me petrol and all what I would want', and I was to wait for him – he would come in his car. I waited. The crowd was most interesting, but most interesting of all were the clothes and hair-dressing and head and face ornaments, etc. etc.

Then proceeded a most amusing pantomime: the old men of the village in masses of long white sheets draped around them, and with large turbans, and each armed with a whip, were those who evidently 'kept order' in the village. These understood from my signs, my plea that the crowd should keep a wide enough circle around the Moth so as not to touch the machine; and the old fellows rushed up and down as fast as they could run, with very high stepping, and hitting out as hard as they could (like Tweedledee and Tweedledum in Alice in Wonderland) at anyone and anything within reach, and at anyone and anything whether in reach or not! They stepped so high, tried to run so hard, and hit out with such huge strokes that what with this and their long and voluminous clothes they nearly turned head-over-heels each time they hit out ... they got into such a frenzy, that I had to be on the lookout and prop them up occasionally when they looked like losing their balance in the direction of the Moth, and diving head-first into it! The crowd roared with delighted merriment at them and didn't mind one little bit if they got hit or not, and I agreed with them that the sight was well worth it!

At last, a Ford was seen arriving down at full speed; scattering dust in all directions, it pulled up very suddenly at the last moment, with all the brakes squeaking and the crowd all cheering, but on such a high pitched note that it sounded like a series of squeaks! And instead of Mr King of the garage, it was what they were pleased to call the King of the village – really a chief of that village – in the most wonderful robes made à la dressing gown, and packed tightly into the back of the Ford, with two interpreters, and a driver in front. He got himself out of this, and I shook hands with him, and proceeded to bombard the interpreters with questions, as to whether that road went to Kano; how far was it to Kano; if they went to Kano by car, and if they could get there in the day … They gave the distance to Kano as under 200 miles, varying to 40 miles – the exact mileage – they said they did get there the same day as they left the village. This village I was told was 'Putuskum'. (I don't even know now if I have put the right name to it). [It is now called Potiskum.]

I asked them to say Thank-you to the King, and say that I would not want petrol, and wished to take off, so they had better clear their street, and keep it clear. I also tried to convey by signs to the crowd on either side that I and the Moth would go slowly down the main street, turn round, and come back fast and go up; and they must keep well back on each side, as it had not got any brakes like the Ford. The latter fact I asked the interpreters to explain: they seemed to understand and kept back; but oblivious to any possibility to danger to themselves, continued to line the streets on each side. I found the sand fairly deep on the part I had to take off on, and could feel my machine skidding about on it pretty well, and by dint of lifting once or twice and trying to really not go casually at it, I kept straight, and took off.

Anyhow, I continued my 'road-following', getting lower and lower as the visibility got worse and worse – then I got to Kano.

I had to fly over the various parts of the town to see if it was right, because I could only see directly below me. After circling around and seeing no white circle to denote an aerodrome, I flew over all parts of the town several times, to try and attract the attention of at least one motor car, to drive out to the aerodrome, and so give me a hint of where this was. But no – not a single sign of life or interest, so then I gave this up, and re-found the race course in the fog, and went down to look at the centre of this. It looked all right, but was soft sand, and I did not know if it had been prepared for seeds or landing ground or what; so, as there were no tracks on it, I went to find another square of ground that I had passed on my way round town. This I could not at once find in the fog. Then I saw some white marks showing in the fog, and I thought, how stupid: that will be it (the Aerodrome) and you have regularly missed seeing them. But on getting closer I saw it was a cemetery! However, next door to this was another level patch of sandy cleared ground, and it looked hard, and there were some tracks on it that looked like those of an aeroplane, so I landed on that, and it proved a perfect piece of ground. A motor car drove up, and someone came running out, and said his name was Carpenter, that he was a South African, owned a Moth, and had it there (and it was the tracks of his machine that I had seen!); that he alone in the town realised it was a strange aeroplane flying over the town, because he knew it was not himself, and everyone else thought it was him!

I sent a message up by a native passing on a bicycle, to ask the police if they would send me down a guard for my machine and three sacks, and to say that I had arrived. After waiting for some time, a message came to say that the 'Boss' was in his office, and we were led to guess that he was likely to stay there! So then we sent up again, and this time the native came back to ask Mr Carpenter and myself to go up to the office and state what we wanted. I sent up again to say that I never left my aeroplane till I had got a guard for it; therefore, would they please send the guard and three sacks. After still waiting – standing in the fog, the native came back to ask me if *I would write a note*, so I said 'yes, I jolly well will' and I sent the following:

'Lady Bailey has arrived by aeroplane, and has been waiting on the aerodrome for three quarters of an hour. *Please* send a guard of four police, with three sacks to tie down her machine, and a car for her to get into town with her luggage. Urgent, please *hurry*.'

This brought a gentleman out at once on a bicycle, and a guard followed, and we filled the sacks, tied down the machine, and a car arrived, and all was well. I had landed on the aerodrome, and there was a white 'T' marked on the ground way off it, hidden in scrum and grass somewhere.

Well, I stayed a day in Kano, and found it all very interesting indeed. A great deal had been done in a few years, and it looked like an experiment of administration that *may* work admirably. There were races in the afternoon, but I had to go and work on the Moth, so I could not see them. I had arrived at the native village [Potiskum] en route, at 10.55 a.m. and had left there at 12.10 and arrived at Kano at 1.30 p.m.

Sunday 25 November

I took off from Kano at 8.30 a.m. with a pretty dense 'Hamataan' in the air. I was accompanied as far as Zaria by the other Moth, flown by Mr Carpenter. I followed the railway from Kano to Zaria, and then on towards Sokoto, and branched off this on to a road, and followed that to Sokoto, where I arrived at 12 o'clock. At the start, I could only see below me when flying low. At Zaria the fog cleared a lot, then got thicker again for the rest of the journey. At Sokoto it was clearer, and also for the last part of the journey.

At Sokoto I saw the aerodrome before I could recognise the town, owing to mist, and they had marked it out most wonderfully. It was surrounded by natives on horseback in the most marvellous clothes, and with the most wonderfully ornamented saddles, and harness of all sorts of coloured leather etc. Some of the horses, which were all between 13¹/₂ to 14¹/₂ hands, were nice-looking little animals. Others looked like a cross, at some period, with those of the old Spanish pictures of wall-eyed war horses, streaked and splodged with streaks of white all over the place; with roman noses, long in the pasterns, hocks right away from them, and a big leggy – though they all seemed to have a fair middle piece – at least, from what little one could see of this, which certainly was not very much. They were hung around like a sort of ambling wardrobe, with their riders clad in voluminous garments, and their saddles with tassels, fringes and ornaments galore hung all around. These riders belonged to the retinue of the Sultan of Sokoto, the fifth most important Mohammedan in the world, whose closed car was there. But as, by his religion, he was not supposed to see women unless they were wearing a veil, as soon as I had arrived, he drove off!

Monday 26 – Tuesday 27 November
I left Sokoto at 8.40 for Niamey, and arrived there at 10.55. I flew a compass course, meaning to come out on the river Niger, between Say and Niamey (to the south); however, I came out directly over Niamey, and landed there. The aerodrome was magnificent as to size, though the wind had blown the sand into long waves of deep sand, with long waves of hard-baked bare ground between, and so, as I landed at each place and felt my wheels stick, I lifted the Moth, and so landed in a series of bounces. I stayed at Niamey for a day, and telegraphed to Gao about petrol and oil, which they replied they had.

Wednesday 28 November – Sunday 9 December
I left for Gao, at 7.40 a.m. I arrived at 10.50. I followed the river Niger. There is nothing much to mark Gao itself, as it consists of mud houses built very close to the river bank, and the aerodrome is hidden till you get almost past Gao (unless you are flying directly over the town), when flying northwards; being a sort of hollow in the ground. However, it shows up well when you do see it, and is a good surface – there is a hangar, as there was at Niamey. Here I thought I should get a good start on for the Sahara, and sent more telegrams to 'Estienne Automobiles' Reggan. I got a reply that they had no motors free to send me supplies, to Ouallen, and at this end what motors existed were going backwards and forwards to Tesalit, or quite close to it, so I could get no petrol or oil taken there.

It is now Sunday 9th December, and I am still stranded here waiting while they telegraph to one another. The houses are of mud, whitewashed over inside, and the whitewash comes off like chalk every time one touches a wall, or one's clothes do. There are no doors or windows, merely openings in the walls with a piece of matting hung over them, which you may or may not be able to roll up. I had a bed with mosquito netting and a mat on the floor, an iron table and a chair, so I was fine. I was lent an enamel basin to wash in, and some towels and bedclothes. Well, now I have been moved, this afternoon, to a house belonging to the schoolmaster, who is away, situated in the native village where the school children repeat their lessons out loud all together, and make a rare din! My other room was at the doctor's house (he is away too), and at night, when I was sitting on my bed there writing all this – as I had to do something, and found this block of notepaper for sale in the town, so started writing this account to interest the family (if they are interested) – an old toad used to sit, half out of his hole in the floor, and croak for quite a long time, and finally come out half across the floor, and croak, and sit there looking at me and the oil lamp. When I shoved him off, he just croaked and hopped most leisurely away and would go into the darkness of the room opening out of mine, to return to the light by the other door, and sit there again, looking at me and croaking! Then a small rat used to come in – they are small and creamy: beige coloured, and look as clean as anything, covered in fur – and he used to sneak about the room from place to place for a while, before finally coming up to have a close look at me! And then when I shooed him off, there was just one scuttle and he was gone. Two swallows were building two nests in the ceiling, but I seldom saw them – they were not so friendly; then by day some tiny birds would come in and sit on the mosquito netting rail and chirp, and talk, and hop about the room. And then at night, a bat sometimes playing here would whizz round the lighted lamp as hard as he could. Really last night I roared with laugher – first I had the toad, then the little rat, and then a large bat, which instead of whizzing round the ceiling, or even level with the lamp, was whizzing as hard as he could round the floor of the room! Flying! And really I did not know if I was seeing things or not … I got a stick that propped up the matting for the door, and had a few hits at him, but as I hit he was always on the far side of the room!

Now, I expect I shall have all the native piccaninnies of the town coming in and out here – or goodness knows if one can't be sure that they aren't here already.

Really, these delays are the very ... And if I wasn't so keen on trying the Sahara, I'd have 'quit this' *long* ere now! Also, I must be an infernal nuisance to them here, as they have to feed me – there being no hotel or anything representing such luxury. There is one store and a tiny shop, and what they do keep is chiefly to sell to the natives, as far as I can make out.

If they will only send me petrol and oil to Tesalit, I am going to try and fly from there direct to Reggan, as they said they could not send me oil and petrol to Ouallen [between Tesalit and Reggan]. They can do that in one day, I believe, by car from Reggan, so I think they might have had the decency! For it makes it a 'far cry' if a wind is against, which is a certainty – but if it blows hard it can leave me with insufficient petrol to reach Reggan, whereas the other would be as simple as cheese!

The situation of the schoolmaster's house is somewhat odorous, being in the centre of the native town, with only holes for windows and doors, which leaves no possibility for privacy. An old native lives on the verandah (by way of keeping guard) and he has a consumptive son with him – at least, by the sound of the boy's cough today. I am to be moved from here again – for which I am very thankful indeed – and if there is any more of this, I shall just get my Moth out of the hangar, fasten it down with sacks in the fresh air and live in that, because this sort of thing is totally beyond my patience.

The French idea of decency is – as is well known – somewhat vague, and they, I am sure, would not even understand if I tried to explain. They have been *most* hospitable and kind, but one can easily discern their open contempt, amusement and antagonism towards everything English. As they hardly do a solitary thing to open up or to assist the natives in their colonies, or spend any money, hardly, on them, they ought not to be allowed to grab another handful of land anywhere, until they have the decency to do some good in what they have got ... They decry the Syrians, and call them all sorts of things, but to me these sound as if they were only doing a more pronounced edition of what they themselves were doing, in fact more lax still as regards moral codes, and even more, after commercial exploitation. I think France – by looks and feelings – will never be either friendly or honest towards England, though individually more than hospitable and kind, etc., as they have been to me here – with the exception that they leave me in a hole and show that they have no intention of helping me out. They are not going to assist my 'raid', and certainly not with any speed – it is of no account to them at all. I know I am jolly sick of it – not a thing to do – stuck by myself, and seeing them 'by invitation at mealtimes'. I have not wished to stay here, but I do want to cross the Sahara, and would like to put a few squibs to these people here!

13

Mary's Flight Journal, Gao to Stag Lane

After fourteen days of waiting in Gao for the French to say they would deliver the supplies of petrol and oil she would need in crossing the Sahara, Mary eventually realized they were not going to help her, and she would have to continue her journey by a different route, along the west coast. She does not comment on the fact that her thirty-eighth birthday, 1 December 1928, was spent in Gao.

Wednesday 12 December
I left Gao at 8.0 a.m. to fly by the coast route via Dakar, as Government facilities to put supplies at Tesalit were refused. I only heard the reply on the 11th, so packed up and took off the next day for Mopti, short-cutting by compass course, instead of following the river up to Timbucktoo. After leaving the Niger River at Gao, one passes over a stretch of not too bad looking country, though seemingly sparsely – if at all – inhabited, till you reach some lakes. I took a compass course to the north of Mopti, to hit the river and to follow it south. I found miles upon miles of inundations, which at certain periods of the year are formed by the river Niger between Timbucktoo and Mopti – some hundreds of kilometres long and about 40 or 50 kilometres broad. The course of the river becomes completely lost in these, and everything is water and waterways, with strips and island of land dotted about among them. There are roads, native villages and one or two places where sheds and work or commerce is being carried on, but all ending in surrounding water, getting submerged. After I had crossed the inun-

dations, all I could see of water clearly on its own was a lake, away to the north or north-west. The visibility in that direction seemed better, but I turned south, thinking I was somewhere near Mopti, and not wishing to go astray, and having no information except a false fact (that Mopti was in the middle of the inundations, which it was *not*). Not having any river to follow, and not knowing the extent of the inundations, I thought I had better find a decent place to land and ask, while I still had plenty of petrol. Finally I chose a piece of land near the first really big road, which looked in places as if it had been newly made up. The patch of ground was not big, and I could not get room to land into the wind: just as I was coming in, I realised that a telegraph line crossed one end of it, and watching to see that I cleared this, I held the stick back a second too long and landed rather short – in fact I dropped on to the ground and bent my axle. It was a wonderful landing ground – level; hard; with only a few stones about; but it was small.

The natives of the village, which was called Goulambo, all came running out, and hid behind the bushes and trees around; however, when I got out of the Moth I beckoned them to come along, and they all did, and shook hands with me. Then, at last, I found one native who had been a 'Tirailleur' of the French Native Troops, who spoke and understood a word of French here and there. Mopti apparently was south of this place and took them four days on foot to reach. I knew that only meant so many hours by car, by road. I got them to understand I wanted the telegraph, and I wanted a motor car – and they got me to understand that I could have a horse and ride to another village to get to a post office and motor car.

I tied down the machine, covered it up, placed a native from the village who promised to guard the machine, and walked with the other natives into the village, and found the chief. He shook hands, and through the interpreter offered me the loan of a horse, to ride to the village beyond the next village, to get the motor car. I was also given some milk in a round basin. I asked for a saddle (not knowing if they had one), and a second horse for a guide to go on, to show me the way. Eventually all this appeared. The saddle had a thing like a pommel back and front, and I wondered how I'd ever succeed in getting on, let alone ever getting off again. The stirrups were flat iron soles, very narrow, and turned up each side, and the stirrup leathers were strands of cords fixed onto the saddle. If you wanted these long you used them as they hung; if you wanted them shorter, you twisted the stirrup round till the cords were all twisted, making it like a rope. It was a jolly little horse and I did enjoy the ride – and the little horse seemed to enjoy it too. I tied up my hand-bag (which had ceased long ago to shut) with string, and put it through my belt, wrapped my dust-coat around the front of the saddle, and proceeded to ride 18 km to Corienza, where I arrived in course.

They have very wicked bits in all these parts, with a beastly high part inside the mouth, that rises right up when the reins on the end of the long curved cheek is pulled, making these horses put their heads up, open their mouths, and travel back on their hocks. The horses were not shod, and the road had had a lot of loose stones put down, so I kept to the side as much as I could, and I let the reins go on his neck. Every time I took up the reins I felt him collecting himself, ready to withstand this beastly bit; and when I dropped the reins on his neck he relaxed again and went along happily. I did feel sorry for the poor little horses in all these countries, and wondered if their mouths ever got hardened to it. The saddle and bridle were all decorated with cut leather fringes, dyed in various colours, which seems the custom among the people all along the south of the Sahara. I was awfully glad to find when we got to Corienza – the village producing the post office and the car – that my little horse, despite all the heat and travelling very nearly the whole way at a hack canter, was not sweating. The native guide's horse was a younger one, but was in a desperate state of sweating and lather, and looking very wild by now as a result of the worrying bit.

I was sorry to part with my little horse, and wished I could have spoken the native language to ask the boy to tell the Chief how much I had enjoyed the ride, but he probably would not have understood why anyone should have enjoyed a ride! I asked that the horses should get a drink and a rest if possible before they went back – and for the guide too.

I found that the new governor-to-be of Mopti was doing a tour of inspection, and happened to be in this village, Corienza, for two days! I met him and his cortège in the main street, and knowing what an apparition I must appear, waited with great glee to see the expression on his face when he saw us. He seemed not in the least shocked or surprised, and was kindness itself.

I went back to the Rest House, where he and Madame, his wife, were camping out, and they borrowed a bed and a mosquito net from the Syrian in the town who had a motor car – and gave me dinner. (I had not eaten since the day before.) I sent my telegram to Mopti, and we all drove out in the Governor's car to see the aeroplane and then the Chief, and returned to Goulambo, where I hired a car.

Thursday 13 – Saturday 15 December
I left Corienza early in the morning. I presented the Chief of Goulambo with a piece of white stuff to make himself a dress with, and then proceeded on to Mopti by car. Here I saw the sergeant mechanic at the aerodrome, who said he would come and get the axle, and put it straight for me. Then I went and saw the Mopti administrator who was leaving, and afterwards got the commercial people and my driver, a Syrian, to get me a room. I then sent off telegrams; got some provisions, and returned to the aerodrome 12 km away from the town. I arranged with the sergeant that it was too late to arrive at Goulambo with any daylight, to work: he said he had to be back early the next day, so I suggested leaving Mopti at midnight, and arriving at Goulambo between 5.30 and 6.0 in the morning to get the axle, and be back in Mopti early, between 10 and 11 a.m. He and the Syrian, owner and driver of the car, agreed to this, and to go to bed early, so as to get some sleep before starting – I did likewise. At 11.45 p.m. I sent a boy to call the Syrian, and was ready myself at 12 o'clock. The car did not arrive, so at 12.45 I sent the boy again, and took my things with me, put them in the car, and tried to wake what proved to be the 'dead asleep' Syrian, who had never offered to get up! Finally, he proceeded to take just about another two hours to get up, pump up a tyre, make some coffee, replenish a gas lamp, and put his tools in the car, etc. ... At last, we got off, one headlight on, one out, and the gas spot-light spitting.

Almost as soon as we started, we ran over a jackal. The Ford was travelling at quite a good speed, and nearly ran over a long length of crocodile, that was hoping to eat the jackal. It was also on the narrow piece of road: it was oozing and drawing its length and fat, spreading middle across the road with a wavy action from side to side, like the slow-motion picture of fish swimming. The driver would not stop, so on we fled to the aerodrome, where we picked up the sergeant and his tools, and proceeded onwards.

We saw no big game – only hares, birds and a few jackals, till morning. They rushed the car off the road at one point, and would have liked to shoot a calf, saying it was a hyena – I only saw a calf, but they had better eyes than I did, and said there was a hyena there too. When light began to come, we got some guinea fowl and a buck. The buck we all shot at and hit, whereas the guinea fowl was chiefly the sergeant's work – he was quite a good shot. The driver tried to run everything down with the car, and would neither stop nor slow down, so we missed getting a good bag of small game.

We arrived at Goulambo, took out the axle, then went to Corienza, where the sergeant heated the axle in a fire and pulled it straight in a vice. Then we picnicked for lunch, and returned to Goulambo and replaced the axle and wheel.

As we were working – I ought really to say while the mechanic was working, as I did little but watch and try to assist – at the replacing of the axle and wheel, the Chief of the village brought me a present of two live cockerels and half-a-dozen eggs. As I had taken up my luggage already by car to Mopti, I had plenty of room, so put them in the locker of the Moth and flew them to Mopti – they both seemed quite happy on arrival, and none the worse for being shut in: I was afraid they might have wanted more air. And so the chickens of the Chief of Goulambo had an aeroplane flight of 40 minutes.

The natives all love a sewing machine, and buy one whenever they can, so the Chief had on his new dress, made overnight out of the piece of stuff I had brought him from Corienza. I stayed two nights in Mopti. On the following day I cleaned the machine thoroughly.

Sunday 16 – Monday 17 December
I left Mopti at about 8.0 a.m. and flew across a very small piece of

the inundations, when the river emerged once more to sight, with a clear course of its own, and started going more westwards. Ségou has a landing ground, but I did not stop there. The country got more civilised as one got near Bamako: at Koulikoro one struck the terminus of the railway line that runs from Dakar. I had been told that there was only a train every 15 days, so had not expected to see one – and I did see one! So much civilisation as this at one fell swoop seemed marvellous, so I had to behave like a baby and go down and fly around and around the train, for the sheer wonder of looking at it.

I arrived at Bamako to find a fairly large town, a big aerodrome, enormous wireless masts, rows of hangars, and a mass of buildings where the troops resided. The town was down by the river, just under some hills which were to the north. Up on these heights were the government buildings, and the Governor's Palace – an enormous building. All these government buildings were daubed with a sort of camouflage colouring.

The Officer Commanding at the Aerodrome I had already met at Gao. He asked me why I had not flown along with them from Gao to Timbucktoo, instead of losing myself? I cursed readily in English, hoping he didn't understand, and said it straight as I could manage in French, that I thought they might have told me that Mopti was not situated in the middle of the floods, but on the eastern edge with a long road running down to it, and that I had not lost myself: I had landed to ask for certain if Mopti was in the floods, and if so, to which side, as if I went on I might get right away from it.

However, my front magneto was not working, and had cut out – I hoped the spring and metal washer of the impulse starter had not bust again. I got a car, kindly provided by the Lieutenant, who said I could not work on the Moth at the Military Aerodrome on Sunday, and that the hangars must be shut again and I must wait until the next day. Waste of a day – still, there it was.

I drove to the Governor's 'palace' on the top of a 'young' mountain, among other houses built up there for the officials of the administration. All of these houses looked imposing edifices from the town, but on approach, they looked like the Hendon display village after the 'burning and bombing turn' is *finished*!!! However, the Governor was away, so I saw his secretary, who had one small eye looking north-east and another small eye looking south-west! He said he would telegraph my arrival, and that I had better put up at the Station Hotel, which he said was the better of the two hotels there. (Needless to say, it was the worst of the two and did not look nice.) Anyhow, I had informed them of my arrival and had asked for advice, etc., so felt I had shifted all responsibility from my shoulders, of the possibility of their cursing me for any particular reason.

I went to the Town Hotel – very nice and a pleasant manager, who arranged to give me a room, lunch, get my clothes washed and get me a car for the following morning early. Knowing I could get food was good news, for I got tired at Mopti with no food, no restaurant, knowing no-one, motoring all night, working all day, and returning after the shops were shut to a bare room at night, without even having any filtered water to drink; surrounded by floods, and my windows opening on to the back doors and kitchens of the 'Commerçants', where I could see their evening meals being cooked. I had hardly any food or water for three days at Mopti: I sent three times altogether to the (leaving) Administrator to ask for facilities, and got none. Finally, on the morning of the third day I went to the shops – when they were open – and the manager of one of them got his wife to give me some breakfast, and my word, what a world of difference it made. But that is Mopti to the traveller, so beware, anyone who wants to pass there!

On the last day at Mopti, while I was working on my Moth, the new Administrator arrived from Corienza and took over my room, as the other Administrator – the one who would not assist me – had not yet left. For the last time I went to kick up a row at the administration headquarters, and they sent me to a youth in the police service, who took me to see some American missionaries in the town (evangelists) who gave me a grand meal at dinner, and a *bath*, and lodged me for the night. I paid the bill for petrol, and asked for a car at 5.0 a.m. the next morning, then packed and slept soundly. Next morning I had a huge breakfast of three eggs, cup of coffee and two slices of bread and butter, and then left Mopti!

Mr and Mrs Howard were the names of these kind benefactors, and they were a contrast to the leaving Administrator, Monsieur Cherron. Well, well I know the French now – lots of red tape, and either they have bad consciences or take everyone for a spy, or else they are up to no good themselves. Anyhow, at Gao they looked at me the whole time as if they thought it must be a great pity *for me* that I was not French, and the longer they did this, the more did I thank my lucky stars that I was not!

At least, my motives were straightforward, and I was but on a sporting tour in a Moth, trying to return to England through their territory. They are either a very queer race – and, as I have remarked before, that as a race they most resemble a capricious woman – or else they are up to no good ... Let it not be forgotten, however, that although this undercurrent of antagonism was there, I had, with the exception of Mopti – which I must say was a *real* muddle, *rotten* muddle – been shown courtesy and great hospitality, and they had made all the arrangements for my reception and lodging everywhere. The trouble began at Gao, and I must try and put it to rights, either here or at Dakar, with them, and have an understanding of some sort – or at both places.

The greatest blow – at Mopti also – on top of being tired and having no food – was a cable to say that Abe had left [London] for South Africa. I nearly howled. But wouldn't have him stay in the cold and get ill on my account for anything. But although I knew this and felt it, it was a great blow. The delays have been very trying indeed, but I felt, having taken on the trip I ought for the sake of the trip to carry it through as, although without any organisation whatever, it was and had been quite possible and I do hope I can manage to carry it through.

My oil is leaking somewhere, but I think it is probably the oil pressure valve, which needs cleaning or attention; and the front magneto is certainly behaving in a funny manner today.

We will work from early dawn at it tomorrow. If no skilled help is available (which I expect will be forthcoming really) I'll get at it myself.

At Corienza there was a black woman fetching water from the floods, and she was followed by a tame, full-grown lamb, washed white sand very woolly; each time she came down for water the lamb followed, waited for her and went off again with her. I thought of 'Mary had a little lamb'. Over the floods was an immense variety of birds of various kinds, and really it was quite wonderful to see them: some of them huge ugly birds but vividly coloured; wonderfully coloured small birds of all sorts; black and white birds shaped like large snipe; long-tailed birds about the size of a woodcock, with every sort of colouring, and heads like that of a miniature parrot; and ducks, geese and storks etc., of all sizes and varieties – as far as anyone ignorant of the details and histories of these birds could judge. Then there were small buck, jackals, hyenas, 'outardes' (or pauw), and all sorts of small game. They also said there were lions and leopards in the country around Gao, but I did not see any tracks or hear sounds of these. Around Gao, Fort Lamy and Fort Archambault they have what they call 'phaucochon' (wart hog), these have small bodies and huge tusks – some of these tusks of great length and weight.

The mosquitoes were bad at Mopti, and also at Bamako, though not so bad here; but the heat was tremendous, and the air very heavy, and sort of suffocating here at Bamako – in fact there seems to be no air at all – anyhow, one has that feeling. I wondered all this afternoon, if this was their winter, what on earth must their summer months be like. It seems very hot at night too, and funnily enough for the first time on the whole journey, instead of the nights being perfectly clear and still and the mists clearing off, there is either dust or dampness – I don't know which – hanging about as soon as it is dark, no matter how clear the day has been.

Electric light has been installed in the town, and in the hotel one keeps hearing whistles which sound like trains; though between Bamako and Dakar there is only one train per week (each way I suppose), but goods trains, I suppose, shunt about locally, and these, I expect, are the cause of the whistles.

I feel as if I have over-eaten today (making up for lost time!!!) and the mosquito netting over my bed is full of holes, but I have so many bites already that I really don't know if I am scratching old or new ones? I found the heat and the mosquitoes getting in through the torn netting too much even for me to sleep with, so finally got up and put the mattress, sheets and blankets on to the other bedstead in the room, and that mosquito netting when I let it down was better, so I slept.

This is the end of Mary's first journal of the South Africa–England flight. After Bamako, the journey is described in three different, somewhat over-lapping accounts that become increasingly patchy as Mary gets closer to London. In what follows I have used passages from all three documents, in order to give as thorough and coherent an account as possible.

Tuesday 18 December

From Bamako I went on to Kayes. Here the Governor and his wife were awfully kind, and entertained me royally. They had a cat with some kittens, and two baby wild cats which she was bringing up as well – two that had been caught in the bush. It was very interesting to see the markings, and the spit-fire ways and habits of these two babies of the wild.

Wednesday 19 December

I went on, and landed at Tambacounda and my goodness, what a rough, hard surface for a light machine; otherwise a good aerodrome cut out of the bush.

From here, on to Dakar. The country between Bamako and Kayes interested me very much. A lot of it looked as if it might be very fertile, but had black soil, and later soil that looked blue. Wonderful rock formation round Dikoa – great flat terraced layers of rock, a good many acres in size, and of a sort of weak sand colour, as far as I can remember. Low bush country up to Dakar.

Dakar the town and port seemed teeming with humanity, very noisy and rather dirty. There seems to be no good hotel there, and I suppose really that the place has not grown and expanded enough to meet the requirements of the port and the trade and commerce of the same. The S.P.C.A. are badly needed here to look after the horses and donkeys working in and around the town. They were scraggy, narrow, shaky specimens of skin and bone; obviously hardly ever fed, and with sores on them – all being worked; and I don't recollect seeing one horse or donkey in a fit state to be working in Dakar the afternoon I was there.

Dakar is the terminus of the French Air Service from Paris, of the Compagnie Générale de L'Aero Postale. Their director at Dakar was grand, and most kind. He introduced me to the bank, to a restaurant, to the petrol and oil stores and the hotel – gave me a chart of the coast route up north; said it was a bit incorrect, but that all the maps of this part were; drove me about in his car, and in fact helped me tremendously, as he saved me so very much time in finding out and searching.

Thursday 20 December
I went on again from Dakar to St. Louis. The air route goes inland over the railway line, where there are forced landing grounds. As this makes a bit of a detour, I thought I'd go by the coast, and cut across the sea. They told me this was the best thing to do: as a matter of fact it was not. When I was out over the sea, my engine starting spluttering, and I shook the machine up, and made straight for the shore. I was not as high as usual as it was cool over the sea for the engine, and I felt I had struck the 'Contre Alysee' winds, at very little height off the ground. I felt as if the gap between the two winds had been at about 250 feet up, but could not say that this was more than a guess on my part. The spluttering re-started two or three times, and then ceased: I think, and thought, it must have been heavy petrol, perhaps as used for the bigger machines. The shore one might have managed to get down on, but never have taken off again from. When I reached it, I took particular interest in it: maybe the tide was high; anyhow, the sand went down in a very steep slope to the water, and was a very narrow strip, and above this were loose sand dunes.

At St. Louis I was kindly driven off from the aerodrome to the Governor's Palace, and given some breakfast. This was an old French house that had been built for the Maréchal de Bouffles who had lived there – it was beautifully panelled and decorated inside.

The town of St. Louis stands on an island; a long strip of sand running parallel to the coast, and the railway and a long bridge cross to it over the water. The aerodrome is on the mainland just north-east of the town. There are no hangars here, but the landing ground is surrounded by lights for the day and night service flown by the 'Aero Postale Cie.'

Going on north from St. Louis, there is a sort of vague track that runs along not far from the coast for a short while, and then there is nothing: water ceases, scrub and grass cease to show up to vary the landscape. The visibility is good, but not fearfully clear – the usual sort of pinkish sand haze is about, and one cannot be sure at any distance what is cloud in the sky or land on the ground.

All is sand and desert; the coast takes on one shape when the tide is out (showing in one place a few tiny sand islands), and another shape, and showing no islands, when the tide is in.

Port Etienne [now Nouadhibou], where I was heading, I knew was supposed to stand on a long promontory of land jutting down southwards into the sea. As I didn't want to go up north and then come round and back again, but wanted to cut across to it when I saw it, I was on the look-out for this piece of land in the sea. Finally, I saw the shape of it away out in the sea, and made for it – only to find that it was a cloud in the sky, that had got, like everything else, a pinkish sand colour. I returned to hit the coast again, and took jolly good care next time to make sure it was land that I flew out to! I did make quite sure next time, and cut across, and found the aerodrome and a hangar, and a gentleman who spoke English like an Englishman. I thought he was English, but he was the chief of that station and section of the 'Compagnie Aero Postale'.

Here again, everything was quite wonderful, not only in the considerate way I was looked after, which was terribly nice of everyone there, but in the way those people started in a place like that to keep their air service running, and for the sake of holding and policing that part of the French desert. There was a wireless, a barracks and a bungalow which served as the living house and mess room and offices of the 'Compagnie Aero Postale'; and I don't think there was anything besides – just the lights for night flying, and that seemed the lot.

Friday 21 – Saturday 22 December
I left in the morning for Villa Cisneros [now Dakhla], on another of the same-shaped promontories. More desert on the way, and no signs of any life. Villa Cisneros was the Spanish station. It consisted

[152]

of a big white fort, with a wireless on top of it, a hangar and a small building where a few officers of the Spanish Air Force reside; and about half-a-dozen old tents, where some very dirty natives they call 'the Moors', who were friendly, live. At this place and at Port Etienne, and also at Cap Juby (north of Cisneros), a few white residents live, without any outside means of communication with anyone, except by the wireless. There are no roads, no grass, no gardens, no trees, no plants, no water and no boat to get away on. (I suppose if they had the latter there would never be anyone there!) Their provisions, including the water to drink and wash in, are brought once a week by sea from the Canary Islands.

On arrival at Cisneros I asked for petrol, as I wanted to get on to Cap Juby; but I was met by one of the Air Force officers, who enquired by whose permission I had come there, and where was my permit to proceed? I showed him my passport, with the visas and letters that I had, but he said that special permission must be had from Madrid to cross any part of Spanish Mauretania, and that I had already crossed a good part of it in coming there. I am afraid that between the two of us we had rather a heated argument; but it was all made up, and I found that without their getting me this permit from Madrid I'd never be allowed to go on.

The Governor and his wife here lived in the fort, and lodged me. They wired to Madrid for the permit. I implored them to try and get Madrid to send an answer through before communicating with London, as I felt sure that would be quite fatal. Ever since Fort Lamy, or some such part of the journey, when I had been presented with a copy of the telegram from the Governor of Nigeria at Kano, which told me to ship my 'plane from Dakar and go home along with it by boat, and that the British would take no responsibility for me if I continued my journey in the Moth, I knew quite well that they would try to stop me somewhere. I knew I ought to be grateful for their consideration of my welfare and everything else, but the chief trouble and anxiety to me was how I could get through ahead of this possibility. So it was again a terribly anxious time, for fear Madrid would ask London, and so mess up the whole thing.

I tried to talk to the Governor's wife in Spanish, by the aid of the dictionary. I learnt about five words of it, such as 'good day', 'good night', 'no' and 'yes', and the Governor and his wife were both quite charming to me, and cheered me up, saying I might perhaps get a permit.

I went for a short walk outside the fort. No-one wanted to walk outside the fort, for everything was sand: the stones and pebbles seemed more sand and shale than stones. I saw a fisherman – a native – among the sandy cliff edges: he got hum, and I turned my walk in another direction. My mosquito boots got the worse for wear here: both soles coming away and flapping; but one of the Spanish soldiers in the fort sewed them on again with some wire (and that lasted out until Croydon).

The permit arrived, and on I went. It had only taken 14 hours to get, and I was grateful to them all for assisting me.

Sunday 23 December

When I took off at Cisneros, the wind was so strong that I hardly seemed to be moving at all. The stretch to Cap Juby [now Tarfaya] was a fair distance [400 miles up the coast]. The weather was said to be visibility not bad, but a very strong wind against. Anyhow, the contrary wind (Contre Alysee) formed at about 6000ft up and at most times on this coast was as strong, so, using this, instead of taking the nine hours I had been told I would, I got to Cap Juby in 5 hours and ten minutes. Until I actually saw the white fort at Cap Juby, I was uncertain as to whether it was Cap Juby or a piece of the coast at half-way between that and Cisneros.

At Cap Juby the aerodrome was all loose sand – the surrounding sand dunes were being blown in from the sea, and that shifted, or 'walked' across the country continually. It must be hard work for them there, keeping the aerodrome from getting engulfed by this continual tide of loose sand. 'Taxiing' on the aerodrome was out of the question. We had to pull the machine, and pull the wheels round, and push, to get it into the hangar. In this place the air was very damp from sea spray. The surrounding country was still all desert, but the sea just here comes in in immense breakers, rolling in one after another, and this is terribly pretty. The roar and rush of this reminded me of the bigger breakers at Muizenberg near

Cape Town: it was exactly the same sound and had the same fascination; watching the sea come rolling and boiling in on to the shore.

Here there were some Spanish troops and officers of the Spanish Air Force, and N.C.O.s and their wives and families. They showed me around the fort, which used to be used by British traders, who lived in a house built on the rocks, just in the sea; till one day the 'Moors' attacked the place when many of the menfolk were away, and murdered the residents.

The N.C.O.s and their wives gave a tea party in my honour, and as far as I can remember I think I tried to make a speech of thanks, through an interpreter. To anyone muddling along on a trip like this, to meet with such kindness and friendliness was a wonderful experience, because it necessarily helped me along so very much, and I deeply appreciated this, not only here, but in every stopping place that I went to. I always felt, and I feel now, that in one way one must have been such a nuisance, and that travelling light, as regards luggage etc., one could not take anything – newspapers or provisions or anything with one; and the continual journeying through such a quantity of stopping places has made it hard even to get all the names and addresses right, just to write a letter of thanks. But I suppose on a flight of this kind it is a bit difficult to arrange for this. I know I am not likely to forget the hospitality shown to a stranger, that was shown to me along the flight out and the return journey.

Monday 24 December
I left Fort Juby in the morning and went on to Agadir. My machine seemed pretty well alright to here.

Tuesday 25 December [Mary makes no comment on Christmas.]
The engine was not firing well this morning, on the front magneto – it sounded to me like plugs, but the mechanic said it was magneto. We had gone over the plugs and magneto etc. together the evening before, on arrival. We finally put in another set of plugs, and the machine fired well enough to go on, but I was just getting over the mountains north of Agadir when the machine cut out. I

stuck the nose down, and it re-started with the throttle full open. But when one levelled the machine to the ordinary flying position, it cut out each time.

I looked around for a dried-out lake I had seen in the mountains a short while before, and at last discovered it, away back under the tail of my machine, as I was very high, just having cut over the edge of the mountains. I went back down to it, and found it was a real landing ground, which was a bit of luck! It, however, did not seem to be near any village or anything else; but it was a pretty place, and I wished I could paint, and had been able to paint a picture of it, and draw the whole scene. A native came up, and said he was the guard of the part, and beyond, and offered, I thought, to take me to a telephone. I could understand nothing further. Finally, as he persistently kept on talking about the telephone I left the machine tied down, and covered it up, and walked off with him.

After walking for about a mile and a half, he signalled me to look at the telegraph lines, which crossed the country just there. I looked at the lines, looked at my guide, then wanted to laugh. However, he walked on, till we came to a little stone hut, very clean and tidy on a hill; there I was introduced to an old man, and a tiny wooden stool was brought out for me to sit on by the door. Then they brought me tea with sage in it, which again was all very clean, in what looked like a pewter tea-pot, and a freshly boiled hard-boiled egg, which I was told by signs to crack against the side of the house on the stones. Both the egg and the tea were delicious. After this, the next act of the play seemed to be for me to go on waiting by the house, while the guard sat out on a bit of a hill, watching for something that was to come from the other side.

The explanation of it all was quite reasonable; even during the short while that the French have been in administration in Morocco they have put large motor-buses on the roads, and one of these was due to pass shortly. In this I could get about 12 kms. Away to the village where the French officials resided, and where there was a telephone. Accordingly, I took the bus to Tamanar, got off there, and went up to explain and telephone. The Administrator's house here was a large one with high rooms, a courtyard with trees and flowers, and a great many steps leading up to it – a most imposing looking building, which had belonged to a chief of the country. I telephoned to the Chef d'Aeroplane at Agadir, who very kindly said he would send out his mechanic on the bus next morning, and the authorities communicated with the British Consul in Mogador, who happened at that moment to be making enquiries about me; as Captain Tattery, who was flying his Moth out solo from England to the Gold Coast, had arrived in Mogador and was asking about my whereabouts.

Mary's day-by-day account ends here. The following are general comments on the engine trouble that dogged her from Morocco to England.

The engine, I must say, puzzled me, as I had, with the mechanic, given it a jolly good clean-over and look-over, the evening before in Agadir, and I was rather at a loss to find any reason except dirty plugs and oil getting up into the cylinders, to account for this. Anyhow, the plugs had been new ones; that the oil was getting on to the plugs seemed evident, and there remained the carburettor. I was, I'm afraid, a bit sick at finding so much trouble, having got back to civilisation; but I was to meet with this from then on, on my way back to London. All I could do on each occasion was to put the machine in order as far as I could. But next morning, on wishing to start, there was always some development which cropped up. There was one aerodrome that let me off not only all right, but that insisted on going over the machine themselves; and there was no question as to how it left that aerodrome. As I had had a fairly strenuous time fiddling about on my own, I thought them all grand people.

The last bit in: especially at Casablanca, I could not take the machine out and get it running in the air in a fit condition to take one. The one thing I was concentrating on was getting the little machine back to London, and the one thing that seemed to be concentrated against me was preventing me doing so! It wasted a lot of time and gave me a lot of trouble, and all this worried me a good bit.

My limited mechanical knowledge had allowed me to deal with the engine when I had it to myself, but what amount of knowledge had I got to cope with mechanics? Personally, I should feel inclined to say it was all due to my own ignorance, but the facts are pretty well against this, and the realisation of it did not give me any confidence, which was just as well, for if I hadn't watched out all along here, I couldn't have got back. It did make me feel mad all the same, and the more determined to coax my way home. It was a pity, as up to here there had been so little wrong with the machine.

At some aerodromes in Spain I arrived on one magneto, or with the plugs missing, or some unnecessary thing. At one place, I asked the gentleman, who kept telling me the engine was all right, to get into the cockpit and run the engine up himself. Then, as I was standing by watching, I saw what was wrong. At one place before the plugs had just been brushed, and never taken to bits for cleaning: here they had been taken to bits, but not tightened up again, and blue lights were making quite an effective display through the loose bits on the plugs. At another place, I found one plug not screwed in tight, and so it went on.

From Casablanca on I had been trying to find warm thick clothes to buy, as it was very cold. The Pyrenees were a great sight in the snow, and all the country was snow from then on to Bordeaux, to Paris and London only a thin layer, but not very warming!

My trip was a muddle through, but there were many unnecessary episodes, and these wearied one a bit. The poor little machine had stood all the muddling, both mine and other people's, and it flew grand still, though it wanted an overhaul. Much of this must be cut out of the story, as it does not do to relate; but there were difficulties beyond my own ignorant muddling.

From her logbook, we learn that Mary spent three nights in Tamanar, the town she had travelled to by bus in Morocco, after her forced landing. Her logbook charts her progress from then on:

Friday 28 December
Flew from Tamanar to Mogador. Flight lasted 40 minutes.
Saturday 29 December
Flew to Casablanca. Flight lasted $2^{1}/2$ hours.
Sunday 30 and Monday 31 December
Local flying in Casablanca.

Tuesday 1 January 1929
Flew from Casablanca to Malaga. 4 hours flying.
Wednesday 2 January
Flew from Malaga to Alicante. 3 hours 20 minutes flying.
Thursday 3 January
Flew from Alicante to Barcelona. 3 hours 50 minutes flying.
Saturday 5 January
Flew from Barcelona to Bordeaux. 4 hours 50 minutes flying.
Sunday 6 January
Flew from Bordeaux to Villacomblay. 3 hours 35 minutes
    flying.
Tuesday 8 January
Flew from Villacomblay to Le Bourget, Paris. 25 minutes
    flying.
Tuesday 15 January
Flew from Le Bourget to Berck. 2 hours 15 minutes flying.
Thursday 17 January
Flew from Berck to Croydon. 2 hours flying.
Thursday 17 January
Flew from Croydon to Stag Lane. 25 minutes flying.

Mary's flying time from Pretoria to London was 124 hours. Her comment on this time was: 'I think getting the favourable winds up at about 6,000 feet along the west coast was a great help, as the wind was very strong against me at times on this coast.' She did not count her journey down to Léopoldville and Angola, as they were not on her direct route. 'From the flying point of view, I suppose my trip was too slow to count as anything wonderful, but as a tour I think it was the most marvellous means of travelling for seeing interesting places, that anyone could wish for.'

Her trip from Spain to Paris was fraught with difficulties. She wanted to travel via Toulouse and Lyons, but she was warned that she should avoid the Rhône valley and the Massif Central, as these would be covered by cloud and fog. Instead she flew east to Perpignan, and followed the Aero-Postale route to Bordeaux. As she looked out of her plane she could see the countryside covered with snow, and the foothills of the Pyrenees blanketed by a thick layer of clouds, with the dangerous snow-covered peaks poking out of the cloud. She had a harrowing trip from there to Paris, because the weather was deteriorating quickly. She was unable to see where she was going, and had trouble finding Le Bourget aerodrome, as her map stopped short of Paris, and the airfield was not shown. 'I looked for it on the north-west side, following the bends of the Seine, but found a great fog bank over Paris which stopped me. [Le Bourget airport is in fact north-east of Paris.] I turned south and worked my way round left-handed until I saw an aerodrome [Villacomblay] where I came down to ask the way. There wasn't a soul about, and by the time I found someone it was really too dark to go on.'

She left her aeroplane there, and got a taxi into the centre of Paris, where she arrived at the Ritz Hotel, her hands still filthy with oil and grease, and her flying coat and boots on. The next day the fog was still too thick for her to fly over to Le Bourget, but she managed it the following day – 8 January.

When she got there she saw that her compass appeared to be stuck.

On investigation it was found to have a bubble the same size as the face in it. Someone kindly filled it up with some pink stuff; then everyone said it could not be swung at Le Bourget. I got out a hand compass I had with me, and we put this on a box, and tried to get north and north-west roughly right by it.

There was fog all the while I was in Paris. The Airways and Air Union machines departed, and either got through or got part of the way or returned, and there I was, stuck every day. If I could have had a shot at it and been allowed to get back into Stag Lane, I'd have felt happier than having to make for Croydon. It was a stupid thing. Anyhow, at last I got off, got as far as Berck [on the Brittany coast] and got into a snowstorm around Boulogne, couldn't see over the channel; could not trust my compass, and so went back and landed again at Berck. Then it blew and snowed. Finally Mr Yonel and Mr Sprigg came over to escort me back. The morning, of course, cleared, and I could see. They came in an Avian, which crawled: they said they were doubtful about one magneto. I kept back with them till over the Channel, by going upstairs and downstairs all the time. Then they took a spurt, and went away up the railway line. I took a course a bit more north; then it was foggy from about Maidstone on to Croydon. I looked about, and saw them again, and was very glad to follow their machine blindly, as at that time I had no very great knowledge of any of the route between Paris and London, and I would never have found Croydon without going to Stag Lane first and coming back to it.

Mary had to land at Croydon, as that was the official ending place for all long-distance flights, and there was a huge crowd of people waiting to greet her there. As she cruised in down the runway the crowd – possibly two hundred people – ran behind the plane until it stopped. There was snow on the ground. The first person to greet her was her mother, who leaned over the plane to where Mary was still sitting in the cockpit, and kissed her. Then Mary stood up in the cockpit, and said 'Where are the children?' Her brother Willie was there too, and so were two of her daughters. It was a never-to-be-forgotten moment for all of them. Mary had achieved an all-time distance-flying record, not only for a woman, but for a human being. No one had ever flown so far by themselves before. She was a heroine: probably the most famous woman in the world at that moment.

Her next act was to fly her aeroplane back to its true home, the De Havilland airfield at Stag Lane, where, no doubt, Geoffrey de Havilland and his wife were waiting to greet her. Then finally she went back to see her other three children, all in bed with influenza in Bryanston Square.

Mary was to write many articles and commentaries on that flight home. One in her own handwriting, scribbled hastily a few months after she got home, makes some general comments:

The main impression of my trip was that with ordinary care on my part how well the machine took me along. That one felt extremely fit from being in the open air so much that the interest of the trip was well worth every minute of it. That the most difficult thing I found was to induce anyone to believe me that it really was alright to allow me to proceed.

The outstanding surprise was finding an excellently run and organised commercial Air Service flying regularly across the Belgian Congo, with British-built passenger-carrying machines, and that this had been running for three years. Also finding another – a French Air Service along the west coast of Africa, from Dakar to Paris, which had been running for eight years. And the sad fact of the non-existence of any British commercial Air Service in any of the British possessions in Africa.

I saw plenty of evidence everywhere of the benefit and the urgent necessity for Air Services, to link up England and Europe with all parts of Africa.

I thought the eastern route, from Cairo to the Cape, a far easier route to organise and run than the one the Belgians and French have each already proved successfully is possible. They are now linking up and developing this, and I do hope England will not delay in establishing an Air Service from Cairo to Cape Town. It is urgently needed, and should be of immense benefit ... my trip I think only goes to show what the aeroplane can offer, and what it can stand up to – from the novice. That with a well-organised route and experienced pilots and mechanics there should be no further excuse on the point of safety and reliability for delay in establishing commercial air routes.

I hope everyone will take an interest in aviation, as it is going to be the chief factor in progress and security.

14

Fame and Folly

The newspapers of the world followed Mary's flight home to England, across the centre and then along the west coast of Africa. Several times, when she landed in remote places such as Goulambo and Tambacounda, and found it hard to telegraph home, she was reported lost. This happened so often that – according to a family tradition, perhaps apocryphal – a cartoon appeared in a London publication of two old gentlemen sitting in their club. One is reading a newspaper, and the caption reads:

'Oh god, what awful news!'
'What news?'
'Mary Bailey's been found!'

In general, though, the press were very enthusiastic. Adulation, praise and honours were heaped upon her from the moment she landed at Croydon on that snowy morning in January 1929, and the press were avid to talk to her. The feeling was not mutual. Her children remember being made to creep out of the back door of Bryanston Square into the mews, during the weeks after her arrival, because half a dozen press cars were lying in wait for her at the front door.

Punch celebrated the landing with a bit of doggerel:

Flying home across the waters
Lady Bailey greets her daughters

With the minimum of pother
As our most experienced *Moth*er.

The pun in the last line almost excuses the awful rhyme.

Mary commented on seeing her daughters at the airport: 'I had a great but pleasant shock when I saw how my children had grown during my ten months' absence. My eldest daughter, whom I always considered quite small, is now actually taller than I am.' Only two of her children – Mary Ellen, the eldest, and Noreen, the youngest – were able to greet her at Croydon. The three middle ones, Derrick and Ann (the twins) and Jim, were in bed with flu. And Abe, in South Africa, was ill too. On 13 January, a few days before Mary got home, Abe had had a minor operation in Cape Town, where he had been for the past month. The *African World* reported on 19 January that he was progressing well and hoped to leave shortly for a visit to Rhodesia. He wrote her a loving letter, dated 7 February, telling her how proud he was of her, and wishing he could have been there to see her fly in to Croydon. She was disappointed he wasn't there, but she knew that the European winter was not good for him, and that he should be back in the warm south.

Her flight was described by *Flight* magazine as 'not only by far the most remarkable feat ever achieved by a woman, but the greatest solo flight ever made by any pilot of either sex'. Admiral Mark Kerr wrote a letter to *The Times* in courtly language,:

I pray Lady Bailey will forgive me for calling attention to her flight, but, though she shuns notoriety, the art of aviation begs for the right kind of advertisement. Speakers who have the progress of flying at heart have often prophesied that in a few more years time people will think no more of flying to Cairo or Cape Town than they do now of going to London, by train or car, to do their shopping; but, though they have said it, in their hearts they did not believe it would happen for a very long time; and here out of the blue, comes a lady who has just flown to the Cape alone, in a Moth, to see her husband, and back again by a new route to see some strange parts of Africa, and with no more concern or pother than if she had gone for a walk in the wilds of Devon.

Without disparagement of other great flights, Lady Bailey, with her absence of plans and preparation, has performed a unique service by 'just flying about' for 18,000 miles and alone looking after her Moth and Cirrus; and by her great achievement, carried out in so ordinary and modest a manner, has advanced the progress of civil aviation more than any flight since that of Orville and Wilbur Wright.

The London *Daily Telegraph* Aviation Correspondent wrote: 'This is the most remarkable flight ever made by a woman of any country.' *The Times* went further: 'This long lone African journey ... will rank as one of the finest and most daring in the world's story of light aeroplane flying.' The dour editor of *The Aeroplane*, C.G. Grey, who was later to cross swords with Mary on the subject of wartime women pilots, wrote more moderately: 'Those who welcomed her, belonging to a generation surfeited with miraculous happenings, were enthusiastic over her pluck, proud of her achievement, and sincere in their admiration that a woman could accomplish the longest solo flight ever made – but they were not astonished.'

On Thursday 17 January, the day after her arrival home, a luncheon was hosted at the Savoy Hotel by the Royal Aeronautical Society, the Royal Aero Club and the Air League of the British Empire. Over a hundred people were hurriedly gathered together to celebrate her return. It was presided over by Lord Thompson, who was the Labour Minister for Air, and also Chairman of the Royal Aero Club. Mary's mother was there, and her aunt Doods; Sir Alan and Lady Cobham; Winifred Spooner; the de Havillands; and the Hinklers.

Sir Hugh Trenchard, who was the 'father' of the Royal Air Force, and later Lord Trenchard, made a brief speech. He said that he felt pleased and honoured to be allowed to support the toast, and that one reason he was able to do so was that neither the Air Ministry nor the Air Force had given any assistance to Lady Bailey. Speaking on behalf of the Air Force, who realized what she had done, he could only say that the flight was worthy of honour. Such flights, which were not assisted by the Air Ministry, appealed to the Air Force very much.

Then Mary herself made a short speech, apologizing that she was not used to making speeches. (This was soon no longer to be true: for the next several years Mary was continually asked to address meetings and luncheons and dinners, and to write articles.) As always, she played down her own achievement. The machine had behaved wonderfully. She knew very little about the engine, but although she fiddled about with it every day it simply kept going. This was the sort of low-key approach she used whenever she talked about herself, and people loved her for it: it was refreshing.

The honours and awards kept piling up. In March she was elected the Chairman of the Ladies Committee of the Air League, replacing Lady Heath. The President of the Committee was the Duchess of Bedford. She started flying at about the same time as Mary, but up until 1929, when she passed her 'A' licence for flying, she had flown as a passenger, her pilot being mostly Captain Barnard. He and the Duchess achieved a flight in 1929 to India and back in under eight days, and in 1930 flew together to the Cape and back in twenty days. She and Mary were to see a lot of each other, often attending the same dinners and air displays.

Meanwhile, Mary had started flying again, as often as possible. She had got a new Moth: a De Havilland Gypsy Moth AAEE. If she could combine flying with demands for her presence at meetings and functions, she did. In May she flew down to Falmouth to open the Spring Flower Show, and at the end of June she attended an International Air Rally in Rotterdam. In early July she competed in the annual King's Cup Race and Siddeley Trophy, which she had competed in before she went to South Africa. She did not do particularly well in it, coming 26th out of 41 starters the first day, 21st the next day and 12th in the Siddeley Trophy race.

In June Abe was well enough to travel back to England, and Mary decided that she and the children would meet him halfway, this time by boat. She took them to Madeira, where Abe's boat stopped for a few days, then they all sailed to England together.

Abe had recently given £100,000 to the Royal Institute of International Affairs, and the Institute had organized a dinner in his and Mary's honour at the Mansion House, at which the Prince of Wales (later Edward VIII and Duke of Windsor) was to speak. The banquet took place on 8 July 1929. The Prince of Wales presided, and was asked to propose the toast to Sir Abe and Lady Bailey. He first paid tribute to Mary:

> Before I submit this toast, I have to say a word about Lady Bailey, who has up till now managed to avoid with typical feminine skill any celebration of her remarkable feat. She has been so quiet about it that it is hard perhaps to realise the scale and the pluck of her achievement. I, like many of you, have flown, or rather been flown, on various occasions, and we are always rather anxious when we go up to see that there is some fairly reliable outfit of maps in the machine; but Lady Bailey did not seem to worry very much about maps, and at one part of her journey her maps could have been contained in what a man calls his waistcoat pocket. They consisted of nothing more than the coastal outline furnished by the Union Castle Company for the benefit of its passengers. But I must point out that Lady Bailey's achievement could never have been possible without a combination of high technical skill and great courage and endurance. Her performance will live long in the history of aviation, and as I once had the opportunity some months back of saying – I am very glad to say it again – Lady Bailey is a very gallant lady indeed. We all wish Sir Abe and Lady Bailey a long and happy life.

He then spoke about Abe.

> Sir Abe has given me a winner or two before now. He has put money on many a dark horse in his time, and he saw such a dark horse in Chatham House [the Institute's headquarters]. Last year he wrote to me saying that Chatham House was exactly the kind of institute needed to realise the ideals of

his old friend Cecil Rhodes, but the most striking thing in his letter was an offer to provide £5000 a year as an endowment for this great institute, and to make the gift perpetual by settling £100,000 for the purpose in his will. How glad I am to accept this offer, and I am as glad tonight to pay my tribute to the public spirit of Sir Abe Bailey which inspired the gift. With one magnificent stroke of his pen he has halved our burden.

Jimmy Thomas, the former union leader who was now Lord Privy Seal in the Labour government, paid his tribute. Then at the end Winston Churchill spoke. He recalled that he had known Abe Bailey for forty years. He was with him in the Boer War and at the time of the founding of the South African Union; and he was in touch with him at almost every stage in the Great War. Through all these stages of South African history, Sir Abe had always worked in one direction, namely, to kill racial hatred and to bring together the great races upon whose co-operation the future glory of South Africa depended.

Abe then got up to make a long speech:

> I thank your Royal Highness for the praiseful and kindly reference to my wife.
>
> My wife believing, in fact she is obsessed with the idea, that the result of the next war will depend on what happens in the air, and that England must be prepared, is devoting her life to flying about England organising aviation clubs …
>
> Air-women are contesting and questioning man's efficiency and supremacy, and no doubt soon we shall be told a man's place is his home, and that the hand-rocked cradle rules the world and must be rocked by him. The coming event, as far as I am concerned, has already happened, and I suppose I shall glide into the next word as the dirigible husband.

He made some interesting comments on the Jameson Raid:

I have had my ups and downs in life ... and my record is, so to speak, known to the police, for one of my 'ups' was when I was locked up in prison owing to my connection with the Jameson Raid, that historical and significant episode, written and spoken of with derision, but when the historian of the future writes the history of that period, he will come to the conclusion that the Raid illuminated the world, revealing the real enemies of England, and resulted in saving the Empire, and for good or evil changing the social, economical and political conditions of the world.

He then spoke of his friendship with Rhodes.

It was my great good fortune while a youth to strike a friendship with Mr Cecil Rhodes, and like the great white chieftain he was, he rests there in the Matopos, his spirit permeating the whole of Africa. He conformed to the religion of Empire which none who knew him could mistake. Look at the map of Africa and see the results of his unfaltering and unceasing devotion to England, the Empire and South Africa. He was a man of peace ... and if he had been alive today he would have been a supporter of this institute.

On 1 January 1930, in the New Year's Honours, Mary was awarded the D.B.E. 'for services to aviation'. She was the first woman flyer to be so honoured. From now on she could be addressed as 'Dame Mary, the Honble Lady Bailey, D.B.E.', which is how Abe addressed her letters when he wrote to her. She now had a hereditary title, a title by marriage, and one which she had earned herself. A month later, Mary was informed that she was the winner for 1929 of the Royal Aero Club's Britannia Trophy, given to the flyer who had achieved the most during the year.

In 1930 Mary and the children escaped at last from living permanently in Bryanston Square. She had never been a town person, and persuaded Abe that they should rent a house in the country; he no longer rented Yewhurst in Sussex. They found the Earl of Jersey's home in Middleton Stoney, Oxfordshire, and rented it from him for three years. It was a large Georgian house with a great portico, and was well equipped with servants. For the first time she and the children could enjoy all the country pleasures they had longed for. They could all have their own ponies, and their own dogs, and the boys could learn to shoot.

From there they moved on to another house in Oxfordshire, Bletchington, belonging to Lord Valencia. This they rented from 1934 until 1940, the year of Abe's death. Jim, the younger son, especially loved his holidays here. He made tremendous friends with the head gamekeeper, Alan Howe, who taught him all about animals and plants and birds and trees and woods. The children joined the local pony club and learned to hunt with the Bicester, which used to meet on the front gravel of Bletchington. Mary hunted with them too. They lived, as did their neighbours and friends, in considerable comfort. Jim and Derrick each had his own butler. One of Mary's grandchildren remembers being told that when the children went out riding they each had their own groom allotted to them – and their one idea was to escape from them and gallop off as fast as they could on their own. This move to the country relaxed them all, and the children remember it as the happiest time of their childhood.

She was seeing much less of Abe, who came to Bletchington only occasionally. The children saw very little of their father when they were growing up, but at Bletchington they saw more of their mother than they ever had before, and felt far happier than they did cooped up on the third floor of Bryanston Square.

There is a letter from Abe at Rust-en-Vrede to Mary at Bletchington, dated 26 January 1932:

My dearest Mary

I must thank you for the cable reminding me to write per Air Mail, as I would certainly have forgotten all about it.

Your letter about the children was most interesting and amusing. I did enjoy the news you gave. They are certainly a bright lot and enjoy themselves – Noreen is indeed a great character, and capable of fulfilling the most optimistic anticipations.

I go out on the yacht when I can and am fishing this afternoon for a couple of hours. I often wish you were here, and enjoying the sea breezes on the bay. I will invite the Malcolmsons down to lunch or dinner at their convenience – we are fewer people from England than usual owing to the fact that it is very difficult to get money out of England to this country. *The loss is* $33^{1}/3\%$. So I have to be careful, and the banks are squeezing us all. – What the end will be goodness only knows. We may all be ruined like the Germans and Russians.

I had the Bernard Shaws to lunch on Sunday. I cannot say I admire him. However he is one of the 'nobs' in literature, and is a play-writer.

M.E. [Mary Ellen] is taking part in an amateur show got up by Lord and Lady Knollys. She is quite good so they say – I can believe it for I saw her act on board ship – I must now close.

With love to you and the children altho they will have left the nest for school.

Your ever loving
Abe.

During this time, Mary had a mission and a message, and she took every chance to write or lecture about it: the necessity of establishing a British commercial air service from London across Africa to the Cape. This was probably the nearest she got to sharing Abe's enthusiasm for all things South African and his belief in the importance to South Africa of its link to England. She knew, from seeing them, how advanced the air links of France and Belgium were, and longed for her knowledge of this to be put to use. Mary's many talks and articles on this theme don't make very exciting reading: they are pedantic and earnest.

Early in the thirties two of Abe's children got married. His son John married Winston Churchill's daughter Diana in 1930. It was a disastrous marriage, and when they were divorced five years later, both sets of parents breathed a sigh of relief. Mary Ellen was married in 1934, and that too was a mistake. Her husband, Robin Grant

Lawson, divorced her the following year, and she immediately remarried, to William Frederick Lloyd. This lasted for twelve years but also ended in divorce. All of Mary's children's first marriages ended in divorce.

Mary was still flying and competing, and setting herself severe trials of endurance. In September 1930 she wrote a description for *Air* of the International Tour of Europe, which had taken place in Berlin on 20 July that year, in which she was one of seven British competitors, all of whom completed the course. There were seventy starters altogether, and only half completed the course. It was a gruelling 4700 miles and included crossing the Pyrenees into Spain and flying north to Danzig.

One of the other British competitors was Miss Winifred Spooner. Mary liked and respected her. She should have been one of the all-time greats among women flyers, ranking with Mary herself, the Duchess of Bedford, Amy Johnson, Amelia Earhart and Jean Batten. But she was struck with a sudden illness when flying in Kenya in 1933, and died the next day. At the time of her death she was one of the very few women flyers to hold a commercial flying licence, and she was certainly the only woman in Britain earning a regular living as the personal pilot to the owner of a private aeroplane. Her boss was a Leicestershire M.P., and never once, although she flew him and his friends thousands and thousands of miles, did she cause him a moment's alarm.

Amy Johnson became Mary's friend in the winter of 1929–30, when they had to learn new navigational skills for their 'B' flying licences. This meant mastering a fearsome list of subjects: Form of the Earth; Maps and Charts; Meteorology; Dead Reckoning; Direction-Finding; Wind/Tide Navigation; The Earth's Magnetism and Compasses; Visual Signalling; International Legislation; and Morse Code. Mary and Amy went to classes at the De Havilland Technical School at Stag Lane. To their delight, their club flying instructors had to do the course as well. In March, a couple of weeks before the examination, Mary invited Amy back to Bryanston Square, so that they could practise their Morse together. Amy wrote to her mother describing the evening.

I enjoyed myself at Lady Bailey's last night! Was waited on by real live footmen! It was great fun. I made several mistakes at dinner but Lady Bailey is awfully sweet and has the art of making one feel perfectly at ease. She's got a lovely house. I'm going again if it can be arranged. We're practising Morse for the exam which is only a fortnight off. I'm very worried about it.

Amy was thirteen years younger than Mary, the daughter of a fish merchant in Hull. She was to cause some angst to Mary by breaking her long-distance woman's solo flying record. She flew solo to Australia and back. The following year she flew to Japan via Moscow and back, and in 1932 she flew solo to South Africa and back, completing the circuit in only five and a half days. After that, with her husband, Jim Mollison, she broke more records, crossing the Atlantic in thirty-nine hours, and in 1934 flying to India in twenty-two hours. In 1936 she again broke the record for a solo flight to Cape Town. Tragically she was lost over the sea when piloting aeroplanes during the war for the Air Transport Auxiliary.

In 1932 a historic photograph was taken of four great aviatrixes at a luncheon hosted by the Royal Aero Club: Mary, Amy Johnson, Winifred Spooner and Amelia Earhart. Mary was the oldest of the four, but also was the only one of them to live on to old age. Amelia Earhart, eight years younger than Mary, was the first woman to cross the Atlantic, in 1928 – she was a passenger – and then the first woman to fly the Atlantic alone, in 1932. She was lost flying over the Pacific in 1937.

Mary did not take her 'B' licence exam until December of 1932. Something else had cropped up. She was asked to help on an archaeological expedition to the Kharga Oasis by a well-known archaeologist, Miss Caton-Thomson. Her job was to be responsible for the aerial photography of the sites. She accepted with alacrity: the oasis was very near the flight route she had taken down from Aswan in the Egyptian desert, and going back there appealed to her. The trip lasted two weeks: Miss Caton-Thompson, going on foot and camel-back, took nine days to reach the site: Mary by plane took one and a half hours. The Egyptian government gave her permission to act as pilot and aerial photographer to the expedition, and she loved it.

Amy Johnson's record flight from London to Cape Town and back was one which Mary found especially challenging – and perhaps irritating. The more she thought about it, the more she wanted to prove she could do it again, and in record time. By the end of 1932 she had started making plans to do a second solo journey to the Cape and back. This time her friend and mentor Geoffrey de Havilland, who had initially offered assistance, opposed the flight when he found out what it would entail. He wrote to her on 29 December 1932.

> Dear Lady Bailey,
>
> I am very worried about your flight to Africa, and would like to again point out some of the difficulties.
>
> To use the machine with its overload of petrol in daylight would not be very hazardous except possibly in the case of a forced landing, but to fly it at night in this unstable condition would be dangerous unless the weather was exceptionally good. In bad weather it might be necessary to fly 'blind' for many hours, and it is very doubtful whether anyone could do this even for an hour unless they had many hours experience of blind flying on an unstable machine.
>
> A forced landing (at least a possibility) at night with an overloaded machine would be very unpleasant at the best.
>
> Perhaps you will think me wrong in writing this letter, or for not mentioning these facts at the beginning. When the big tanks were contemplated I did not realise the flight was to be a record attempt involving night flying at a bad time of the year, and it is only when thinking much more about it that one realises the risks involved.
>
> In the early spring, weather would be better, days longer, and you could have flown the machine more with various loads. Is it quite impossible to consider this?
>
> I hope you will forgive me writing like this, but we cannot help thinking of your well-being.
>
> Yours sincerely,
>
> G. de Havilland

He obviously knew what her reaction would be. She wanted to go and she was going. He was right, and was proved right, but he could not stop her.

On 13 January 1933 Winifred Spooner died in Kenya. On 15 January, at the coldest moment of the winter, and at the unearthly hour of 2.35 a.m., Mary took off from Croydon in her new silver Puss Moth, to try to beat Amy Johnson's record.

She had an extra fuel tank, as before, and could as a result fly for twenty hours without stopping. But to save weight, she had no radio (batteries were heavy), no navigation lights, not even a dash-light on her instrument panel. If anything she had done before was foolhardy, this beat it. This was foolhardiness in the extreme.

She reached Oran, on the north coast of Algeria, safely. In her new Puss Moth she could travel much faster than in her old X Moth, and she had crossed the Mediterranean with no trouble. In Oran she re-fuelled, and continued on the second stage of her flight for 1500 miles, until her petrol tank was almost empty. She then had to force-land in the desert, at Ortahuoa, twelve miles south-west of Babau, and not far north of the southern edge of the Sahara desert. She was completely stranded, and for four days no one knew where she was. Mary left no account of these four days, but apparently she was guided down to land by seeing the lights from an Arab encampment in the desert, and landed down beside them. They were probably some of the tribes the French authorities had been trying to protect her from when they refused to let her leave Gao. Eventually she was spotted by a French reconnaissance plane, which had been searching for her for days, and a caterpillar tractor was sent to pick her up, and later returned with fuel for the aeroplane. The next day she was able to take off again. But she had had enough. She decided to return to London.

C.G. Grey, editor of *The Aeroplane*, was scathing about her attempt. 'Whereas the Honourable Mary Westenra when hunting some years ago could have broken her neck without harm to anybody bar grief of the many friends of so charming a personality, she cannot now as the Honourable Lady Bailey go and die in the Sahara or be drowned in the Mediterranean without very great harm to the sport of flying. In the best interests of British aviation she should not have undertaken this journey.'

And what, meanwhile, of her husband and children? Her son Jim remembers the crisis well. On the fourth evening, when there was still no news of her, the five Bailey children were taken to the pantomime in London, to try to distract them from their worry. He tells the story:

> … we were sitting in the audience and the play was going on, and there was no way they could have known we were there, but the news came through on the wireless that Lady Bailey, who had been missing for four days in the Sahara, had been found by the French administration; and so the comedian stopped the show, went to the front of the stage, and announced to the public that Lady Bailey had been found safe and sound in mid-Sahara, and then the chorus broke into 'The camels are coming, hurrah, hurrah!'

She had a horrid time flying home. Her spirits must have been at their lowest, and the weather was as bad as it could be. She got to Alicante, on the east coast of Spain, and was stranded there by fog. In spite of all this, she managed to write a funny letter to Jim from the Hotel Palace in Alicante, dated 28 January 1933 – one of the few of her letters that has survived:

> Darling Jim, Here I am stuck for bad weather reports ahead of me along coast here overland and sea. But as the upper clouds appear to be perambulating in the opposite direction I think that the upper air wind has changed although the surface wind is the same still, but I think if the wind has changed perhaps the weather may also by tomorrow and let me get away from here. It is dreary work waiting here with nothing to do – I am so longing for news of you all to know how you have all been getting on and all your news and how Willie [her brother] is – I have still got the flue I caught off him and cant shake it off. All this coast must be quite lovely when the sun is out. They have the most wonderful tangerines here that are grown in Valencia a little further north along the coast. Every door in this hotel squeaks simply ter-

rifically and a family with a baby who does the same in much the same tone has arrived today so its rather like an orchestra playing along the passage – the baby is winning hands down at the moment … they have lots of horses here and sometimes they are tandem horse and mule or a mule and a donkey or a horse and a pony – there was one team this morning of 2 horses and 2 mules put alternately and singly one in front of the other – the drivers seem to tie the reins up and go to sleep on the floor of their cart and leave the horses mules donkeys ponies or whatever is drawing the cart to get out of the way at the sound of a motor horn, of their own accord, and I must say that they do seem to do this.

The letter goes on like this for seven scrawly pages, and eventually ends: 'Well just tons and tons of love and hope very soon to see you yr loving Mammie.'

She did not arrive back in England until 14 February, seventeen days after this letter was written. The weather conditions were appalling all the way back. Soon after she got home, she was seriously ill with typhoid fever.

There are no more records of Mary doing any long-distance flying after this date. Perhaps Abe was at last able to put his foot down. That great and glorious time of her life was over.

15

After the Flying Was Over

After Mary gave up competitive flying it must have pained her to watch younger flyers making and breaking new records every day. The aviation bug had even spread within her family. Her brother Dick twice won the King's Cup race – which Mary never managed to do, although she took part in it many times. And Dick's wife had taken to flying as well; in 1932 she had made the very flight to Cape Town and back that Mary had done, albeit not solo.

From now on, the only serious risks Mary was taking were in the hunting field. She was left more and more to her own devices. In 1932 Mary Ellen, who was then nineteen, had gone out to stay with her father in South Africa. It was the first time any of Mary's children had been there. Ann and Noreen were at school in Malvern. Her sons, at Winchester, complained to her that they were hungry in the evening, so she conducted a campaign against the Governors, which she eventually won, forcing the school to put on an extra meal of High Tea at six. Now, in her forties, she cut a formidable figure. Her face was prematurely wrinkled as a result of smoking fifty to sixty cigarettes a day. She didn't mind. Her appearance was of little importance to her, apparently. In a series of adulatory articles in a French newspaper after her African flights, the writer notes with amazement that she travelled 'sans boite à poudre'.

While Mary suffered mentally after the end of her flying career, Abe was suffering physically. In 1936 he was forced to return to England for treatment of his arthritis, which had rendered him lame. While he was in London he was diagnosed as having what was then called Berger's Disease, now known as Peripheral Vascular Disease – blockages in the blood vessels leading to the extremities of the limbs. Because of the acute pain, and the possibility of gangrene, one of Abe's legs was amputated above the knee.

He still went racing, took an interest in his stud at Newmarket, pursued his business interests, and commented on international affairs. But the disease did not cease with one amputation, and in 1938, in South Africa, it was found necessary to amputate his other leg. Mary flew down to be with him for the operation. He was able to joke that it was appropriate that he should leave one foot in England and one foot in South Africa – and indeed the photographs of him being trundled out of his specially altered Rolls Royce on a stretcher, arriving at Bryanston Square, show his eyes twinkling merrily.

He had returned to England to attend the coming-out ball held in 1938 for his beautiful youngest daughter, Noreen, who was seventeen that year. He is remembered by people who were there, sitting at the top of the great staircase, as the guests came up in a queue. One poor debutante remembers that he noticed her quietly edging her way up the side of the queue to get to the front. When she was almost there, Abe suddenly bellowed at her 'Go down to the back!' She slunk down again totally abashed.

Abe was still actively interested in politics. Though he remained a firm supporter of British imperialism, he had come to realize the limitations of forcing colonized peoples to participate in European conflicts. In a farewell speech to the South African press, at the time of Mussolini's war in Abyssinia in 1936, he discussed this:

> The abolition of slavery, with its immense vested interests, is the brightest achievement in the record of the British and American peoples. I venture to predict that the organisation of the Negro races by the powers of Europe into conscript armies, will in the end prove more disastrous to Africa and the world at large than slavery itself, and it may prove even more difficult to stop, once it has begun.
>
> The conscription of black peoples by white governments

is the revival of slavery in its most dangerous and subtle form.

Abe was less perspicacious in his assessment of the Munich Crisis. In October 1938 wrote a letter to *The Times* applauding the stance of his friend Neville Chamberlain:

> Sir, on the eve of my departure for South Africa, perhaps you will allow me to give my impressions of the crisis through which this country has passed and some conclusions I have reached after consultations with some of my overseas friends concerning the future international policy of the British Empire.
>
> The British people in the last few weeks have experienced a great awakening to the meaning of modern war. They were calm and determined and ... proved again that old axiom that the Englishman is at his best when he is boldly led and is told the truth and is put up against it.
>
> The crisis brought forth the man. Neville Chamberlain, 'the peacemaker', averted war and saved the world. I tip my hat to him. He is the hero in the mind and eye not only of England but of the Empire. He got past the barricades of Dr. Goebbels and proved to the world that the German people are beginning to think for themselves, and their thoughts are turning not to war but to peace. ... Let us all strive ... to make real friends with Germany. Friendship and co-operation between Great Britain and Germany is essential to peace and to the maintenance of civilisation.

Less than twelve months later Germany and England were at war. A letter at the beginning of 1939 from Chamberlain to Abe shows how blithely unaware the Prime Minister was of what was to come.

Abe's disease, which caused him acute pain, was not halted by the two amputations. In 1940 he was told that he should also have his arms amputated. He firmly said that he would rather die. In the last months of his life, in Muizenberg, his chief pleasure was going out on his yacht *Clewer*, and taking neighbouring children out with him. Mary could not travel down to the Cape in wartime.

During the last seven months of Abe's illness, he was busy writing letters and sending parcels of fruit to his friends. Most of his papers were destroyed after his death, but one packet, all written in 1940, has survived, and the letters – from Chamberlain, Margot Asquith, Lord Elibank, and others – have been collected by his son Jim into a book. The most striking thing about these letters is that at least thirty of them are thanking Abe for something. Twenty-five of them, all from England, thank him for fruit; Chamberlain thanks him for cigars, and later fruit; Sir Patrick Duncan and his wife – he was the Governor General of South Africa in Pretoria at the time – thank him for venison. There is a letter written in April telling Abe what a splendid party he had given the night before. The last letter in the collection, dated 5 August 1940, from Sir Patrick Duncan, starts with the sentence 'I am glad to hear from Hennessy that you are on the mend.' Abe died five days later, on 10 August 1940.

It was the bleakest and most perilous time of the war, when the Battle of Britain was at its height. Abe and Mary's two younger sons were fighting. Derrick was serving as a second lieutenant in the South African Irish Regiment, and later became a captain in the South African Air Force. Jim went into the Royal Air Force and became a fighter pilot in the Battle of Britain. Both were awarded the Distinguished Flying Cross for bravery.

Abe was buried high on the cliff above his house, Rust-en-Vrede, on a level platform of ground he had specially chosen for its wide views on all sides, of surrounding bays and far-off mountains. To reach this remote eyrie, his coffin had to be carried down from above, down a hundred precipitous stone steps.

Abe's last will and testament had been written in November 1937, in Bryanston Square. He left the bulk of his fortune to be administered as a trust. In setting out the aims of this trust he was leaving behind him an expression of his own philosophy and beliefs – a nutshell exposition of all that had motivated him during his life of public service to South Africa. The third clause goes as follows:

I, being a South African, am desirous that the South African people shall in increasing measure progress in numbers, in capacity, and in a spirit of national unity in membership of the British Commonwealth of Nations, so as to take a place among the peoples of the world benefiting their past history and the resources with which our land has been endowed. It is my firm belief that the attainment of this end will depend upon the two parent stocks, British and South African Dutch, of the European population; on their ability to maintain and reinforce the stocks from which they have sprung, to hold and strengthen their position in agriculture, in industry and in business enterprise, and to work together wholeheartedly in devotion to the interests of their common country.

For this trust he left a quarter of his estate, or £500,000, whichever should be less, to be invested in the Abe Bailey Trust. He appointed six trustees: one was General Smuts; one was his son Derrick. Eighty per cent of the trust was to be spent in Africa.

One clause specified that 'native and coloured persons should not be excluded from any benefit under the trust'. Another, rather curiously, stipulated: 'Inasmuch as I hold the view that any religion which precludes or prohibits a marriage between one of its adherents and a person of a different religious faith is not a true religion, I direct the said Trustees not to apply any part of the funds of the trust in assisting any person whose religion precludes him from marrying anybody … outside his faith.'

This trust was to be administered during the ten years following his death – he did not wish the sum of £500,000 to be withdrawn suddenly from his business, which he wanted his executors to carry on for him after his death. He hoped at least £6000 per annum would be available from his business to be spent by the trust.

The trustees were to be responsible for as Abe's fine collection of pictures, mostly in Bryanston Square. He wished this collection to be given in its entirety to the New Art Gallery in Cape Town – 'subject to suitable accommodation being provided for their housing and display, to the satisfaction of my executors. If possible I would like them to be exhibited as a whole, under the name "*The Abe Bailey Collection*".' The bulk of the collection is made up of sporting pictures: oils, watercolours, etchings and prints, which Abe had lovingly assembled through the years. But as well there is a Gainsborough; three Stubbses; three Reynoldses; two Hoppners; three Peter de Wints; a Turner; an Orpen; eight Morlands; six Munningses, all of Abe's own racehorses; three Raeburn portraits; a Ruisdael; and four portraits by Romney.

In the National Gallery in Cape Town there is now one large room entitled 'The Abe Bailey Bequest'. In it are hung some of the finest pictures: the Gainsborough, a Reynolds, a Stubbs, a Lawrence portrait, a Munnings – thirteen of his pictures altogether. The rest of his paintings are not on view, due to a lack of space.

For some years Abe had been giving money to the University of Stellenbosch, and he left it money in his will for scholarships. The Royal Institute of International Affairs was to get £5000 a year for ten years, and also his portrait by de Lazlo. He left money to his old school, the Keighley Trade and Grammar School, for an Abe Bailey Scholarship.

To Mary he left 'during her life such a sum in each year as together with the income which she shall receive in each year under the trusts of any settlement executed by me in contemplation of or since our marriage shall provide her with an income of ten thousand pounds per annum'. £10,000 per annum – the equivalent of almost £400,000 a year today.

To his two sisters he left money to provide them with an income of £1500 a year. To his son-in-law, Dr William Francis Christie, married to his eldest daughter Cecil – she met him while she was nursing at the end of the Great War – he left £500 per annum.

Several codicils, added in 1938 and 1939, remembered other organizations and individuals: the South African Boy Scout Movement, Princess Mary, the nurses who cared for him in the last years of his life, and many others. One amendment, which attempted to safeguard his children's inheritance, led to difficulties:

> Owing to the unhappy state of affairs at present existing in the world and the impossibility of foreseeing what effect they will have on the fortunes of individuals, and in as much as ... my children will only inherit after all Trusts, legacies

and annuities are provided for; I feel it is necessary for me to make reasonable provision for the members of my family in priority to such Trusts, legacies and annuities. I therefore desire to amend my said Will as following: ... I recommend that my executors should not realise my estate until a period of ten years shall have elapsed after my death, in order that the position of my estate may be consolidated during that period.

This seems a perfectly straightforward directive, and had it been followed, there would have been no trouble. The next sentence, however, seems to cancel this directive out.

On the other hand if in their discretion they consider it advisable to realise any asset, including my house with its grounds styled 'Rust-en-Vrede' and the furniture therein, then, notwithstanding anything contained in my said Will they may realise such asset.

Abe thereby left it to the discretion of his executors to decide whether and when they should sell off his assets. Because the executors were prominent figures, they were not always available to spare time to handle Abe's affairs. As a result, the estate was handled badly: assets were sold off immediately after Abe's death, at bargain prices.

Mary's inheritance was not affected by all these shenanigans, but naturally she worried about her children's inheritance. She gave Jim great support in his efforts to sort out the will, and eventually moved down to live in Cape Town to be with him there. This was something she had never been prepared to do for Abe.

16

Last Years

Abe had died in Cape Town on 10 August 1940. Mary, at the beginning of that year, had seen a new role for herself: to help the war effort by putting all her valuable experience as a pilot to use again. She applied to become a pilot in the women's section of the Air Transport Auxiliary, and was accepted. The A.T.A. had been formed in September 1939, and by January 1940 eight women had been taken on. Their chief duty was to deliver new aeroplanes from factories to Royal Air Force squadrons. Another woman who worked for this organization, and who later lost her life over the English Channel while flying for them, was Amy Johnson.

As usual, any flying by Mary caused excitement in the newspapers. At the beginning of 1940 she and another woman, Lois Butler, flew their first Tiger Moths from Hatfield aerodrome, where the ferry pool was situated. But Mary only worked there for one week. The article implied that although the age limit for woman pilots was forty-five, Mary, because of her wealth and her influential husband, had been allowed to break this rule. Under fire, Mary had to give up the ferrying. It must have been a bitter decision. She wrote an indignant letter, saying that women's potential was being wasted, and there were millions of women who could do a useful job in wartime. She herself had had experience as a driver in France in the First World War, and knew how valuable her work had been. Three months after this, eight more women were taken on to be ferry pilots, Amy Johnson among them – but she was much younger than Mary.

Mary's disappointment was compounded by an extremely nasty letter written by her old enemy, the editor of *The Aeroplane*, C.G. Grey:

> We quite agree with her that there are millions of women in the country who could do useful jobs in war. But the trouble is that so many of them insist on wanting to do jobs which they are quite incapable of doing. The menace is the woman who thinks she ought to be flying a high-speed bomber when really she has not the intelligence to scrub the floor of a hospital properly, or who wants to nose round as an Air Raid Warden and yet can't cook her husband's dinner. There are men like that too so there is no need to charge us with anti-feminism. One of the most difficult types of man with whom one has to deal is that which has a certain amount of ability, too much self-confidence, an overload of conceit, a dislike for taking orders and not enough experience to balance one against the other by his own will. The combination is perhaps more common amongst women than men. And it is one of the commonest causes of crashes, in aeroplanes and other ways.

Mary's next step was to join the Women's Auxiliary Air Force as a non-flyer, and she remained in it throughout the war. It must have been hard for her to endure being told what to do by women far younger and far less competent and experienced than herself. But she stuck it out. A letter to Jim dated Sunday 7 June 1942 shows how infuriated she sometimes became:

> Darling Jim – We have had 2 baking hot days and today quite cool again – I do hope you are alright – and are fit and well and getting proper food and rest. I misguidedly said I would go to Church parade this morning which resulted in being assembled at 9.30 and getting to Church at nearer 12 noon than 11 a.m. in a theatre on the furthest-off pier. We had to wait and wait and then they muddled all the flights and squadrons up, and dispenced with all the good NCOs

and left the lot in charge of a pallid puffy dumpy fat Waaf sergeant with dyed auburn hair which got more and more untidy as the morning and our sense of proportion wore through. She got mixed up herself and put the step wrong all the time. We then picked up a Waaf band who beat the time and to which no-one paid any attention and on top of all this they like 'all the king's horses and all the king's men' marched up miles and marched back again and not content with once but covered the town length by streets and parades again and again and finally paraded this muddle the whole length of the sea front to the furthest pier – Never never have I seen so much stupidity about 3 or 4 Waaf officers who had not the gumsion to see what a thorough rabble and rample the whole show was.

Another of Mary's wartime letters to Jim, dated 3 December 1944, shows a late-flowering maternal streak:

Darling Jim, How are you? I do hope well – I got with your coupons for you at Harrods as my Xmas present (or part of it) to you 2 prs unshrinkable pants size 38 and 2 long ditto vests and one pr or 2 prs thick grey wool stockings. You will have to turn these down but they were the only things I could find that looked as if they would last you 5 minutes. I have 2 of your coupons left but Harrods had rotten shaped very thin wool socks so I thought those would be just holes after a few minutes of yr wearing them I'll try to get some wool but that seems very difficult to find also – but I'll have a try and then see if I can farm out the knitting so that they wont take such a long time …

In the same letter Mary urges Jim not to 'go in for Transport Command just as I've got you out of the strain part of it' – a reference to her successful plea to her husband's old friend Winston Churchill to grant Jim a period of rest after his harrowing experiences as a fighter pilot. Jim was allowed to leave his unit for a while, thanks to Churchill's intervention, and was thus able to regain his equilibrium. (Jim published a book of poems about his experiences as a fighter pilot in 1993.)

As soon as the war ended, Jim felt it necessary to go down to Cape Town to look after his father's affairs. When he discovered how badly he was needed there to take control of what was happening to Abe's assets, Mary realized that there was scope for her to help him there. The house at Bryanston Square had taken a direct hit from a German bomb during the war, and was completely demolished. When this happened, Mary found a house in Oakham, Rutlandshire, called the Stud House – perhaps named by Mary after her parents' Grace and Favour residence. This became their wartime home. But soon after Jim moved to Cape Town Mary went down to join him and bought a house in Kenilworth, a suburb of Cape Town, called The Mains.

In 1946 her brother Willie and his wife Dot decided they must move out of Rossmore Castle. It had become infested with dry rot, and Dot had never liked it anyway – she preferred Camla, the fine Georgian house on the estate near the castle. They held a sale of furniture in 1946, and Mary went over and bought some things for her house in Cape Town. The most spectacular objects she bought were the two great bronze statues of Russian horses and riders which had stood in the hall at Rossmore. These she put on either side of her door on the garden side of her house, and they looked magnificent. This pair of childhood friends must have comforted her in her exile.

She spent more and more time in South Africa as she grew older, only occasionally going back to Europe. She often went to the aerodrome, Young's Field, at Wynberg, the scene of her spectacular arrival that day when Abe waited so tensely for her, in 1928. She loved watching the new planes taking off and landing.

Denis Hennessy, the former chairman of the Bailey Trust in South Africa, remembers a bizarre lunch he had with Mary in London after the war. He was staying in the R.A.C. Club, and Mary invited him to come and have lunch with her in St James's Square. During lunch, she took an extreme dislike to one of the waitresses. For some reason she decided this waitress had put 'the evil eye' on her, and she told her so, eventually reducing the waitress to tears.

Denis Hennessy, a young man at the time, was acutely uncomfortable. It was the same sort of agony that Mary's children used to feel when they were little and had to go shopping with her, and she was unbearably nasty to shop assistants.

Jim was extremely grateful to have Mary's support. Later, after he had finished sorting out his father's affairs, he went into publishing, and started the famous *DRUM* magazine, which rapidly became a most important – and controversial – publication, catering to blacks in Africa. In recognition of this work Jim was awarded the C.B.E. in 1996.

'When I was in publishing I was up against the government in a terrific way,' he recalled. 'To have someone as prominent as my mother behind me gave me a great feeling of confidence.' Jim could rely on Mary being prepared to use all her influence, which she surely had in high places up to the time of her death, to help smooth his path.

Mary's mother Mittie died in 1953, at the age of ninety-two. Her aunt Doods lived to a splendid old age as well, still hunting when she was over eighty, but Mary was not destined to live so long. She developed lung cancer in 1958, at the age of sixty-seven. In typically courageous fashion she fought the disease for two years, still travelling back and forth to England, but by commercial British flights, of course, by then. She had plenty of dogs, and her daughters came to stay with her – not always happily.

A doctor, Rex Wilson, who knew her when she was dying, has left a poignant account of his visits to her. He was interviewed some time later, and asked what he could remember about her, and his comments are penetrating and sad.

> I went to see the old lady, and she was obviously very ill. We started off on a very straight footing because I asked her when she would like me to come, what would suit her, and she asked when I did my calls, and I said 'I start at 8 in the morning, sometimes earlier' and that would be a good time if it suited her. 'Yes,' she said, so I go then, on the first call, and the butler, a very charming black chap, came down and said he would tell her. She was in bed, and she sent down a

message to say that she would not be available for some time. So I sent up a message saying that she had made this appointment and I was here now and she was to get on with it, or forever hold her peace, and she could get plenty of other doctors if she wanted them.

Luckily she loved this, because she was the same kind of person. She said, 'by all means come up', and so there she was in bed, trying it on, obviously, a sort of 'Grande Dame' seeing if she could put me in my place.

She said, 'Won't you sit down?' so I sat on the edge of the rather large bed, and she had some lovely big photographs of the children. I said 'are those your children?' and she said yes. So we started talking, and I said 'Tell me about them,' and she said, 'What about you?' And we started talking about our children. And that was a good start.

Of course when I examined her the diagnosis was that she was desperately ill – she had a spread of the cancer in her lung and she had fluid on the outside of her lung. And so I said to her, did she understand how ill she was. She said no. So I said, 'Well, your condition is very serious, and normally one would do so and so and so and so, and we would take the fluid off the lung, and we would keep you comfortable and pain-free', and the main thing was for her to tell me loud and clear what she needed; and I would serve her, and that it was an enormous privilege to be with her at that time of her life, and that she was not to think that because she was so ill there was not plenty that we could do together as doctor and patient – really opening up the opportunities for her to talk about any anxieties – the normal anxieties one has.

I was very fond of her. She was a straight as a die, and if she didn't like it she let me know. She was a very straight communicator. She was very demanding, probably spoilt because of her wealth; second because she went on and on and on being head of the family when her husband died, and I don't think that, apart from Jim, they were very assertive. She had firm opinions about everything. She was brave and straight and uncomplicated in those practical things.

The way in which her children were raised was the norm in families like hers, and don't forget she was probably brought up that way herself. Despite the fact that certain of her children had problems that were well known in the circles in which they moved, I didn't get the information from her. And it is a very nice memory of her, of the pleasure and joy that she had from all her children. On that first visit we had established that mine were very important to me and hers were very important to her. All the things that she recalled about her children were positive, they were very loving, and there was not much of this 'if only' stuff. But then I think that was because she was a very well integrated human being – but then you would have to be, to stand that marriage. (We never discussed her marriage, mainly because I should imagine there wasn't one.) The two things that came through to me strongly as positive things were her childhood and the life that she had in Ireland, and the fact that her children were very dear to her, she loved them.

We never discussed her girlhood. We talked only of her childhood, which may or may not indicate that we were leading up to a part of her life which was a negative thing.

I have very positive good memories of a very powerful brave human being. She was one of those powerful, brave, gutsy, loyal human beings, and I would like to say that she is great.

Mary died in August 1960, three months before her seventieth birthday. Rust-en-Vrede had been sold – first to the owner of a tea company in South Africa, and later to a Captain and Mrs Hampshire. The house still looks very much as it did in Abe's day. Mary decided, before she died, that she would like to be buried at Rust-en-Vrede, in the same place as Abe. Although in life she wasn't able to give him the love and support a wife is expected to give her husband, after his death, as seems to happen so often, she understood much better how much he meant to her. She did not want to be buried in her own Irish bogland. Living her last years in South Africa, perhaps she understood more and more how great a man Abe had been – and in the end she was glad to be buried beside him. The stone erected to her has engraved on it a picture of one of Mary's international flying trophies. It has two figures, a man and a woman, with outstretched wings – the man above the woman, and the woman kneeling on a globe, which is encircled with clouds.

The stone plaque leans against the low wall, and all around the sea and the mountain ranges stretch far away. Since her death, two of their daughters have joined their parents here – Mary Ellen, who died only seven months after Mary, in March 1961, and Ann, who died in December 1979.

Nearly forty years after her death, there are not many people alive who knew her, and very few who remember the flying feats of this remarkable woman. And yet there was a moment, in January 1929, when she was the most famous and most talked-about woman in the world. She deserves to be remembered most especially and enduringly for those pioneering flights to and from South Africa; and for her later campaign to join South Africa to Great Britain by a commercial air route. The first flight by Imperial Airways, in January 1932, from London to South Africa, represented the realization of Mary's dream, for which she worked so hard.

APPENDIX

Mary's Paternal Ancestry

The custom in most large Irish country houses was to fill the dining-room wall with family portraits, and Rossmore Castle was no exception. Mary's ancestors looked down on their small descendant from a variety of interesting portraits, some of the earliest being Mary's Dutch ancestors, who emigrated to Ireland from Holland as merchants in the early seventeenth century, during the reign of Charles I.

Their name was Westenra. This was an adaptation of the name Wassenaar, which still exists in Holland today, and whose roots go back to Philips van Wassenaar, who died about 1225. The family had gained fame in a campaign fought by the Dutch against the Duke of Alva. The first Westenras in Ireland were the brothers Derrick and Warner, and Derrick's son Peter. They did not live in Monaghan, and the title of Baron Rossmore of Monaghan was not created for the Westenra family, but for a General Robert Cunningham, in 1794.

General Cunningham was Scottish. The Reverend John Scot wrote in 'A Review of the House of Commons 1789' that General Cunningham's voice was 'clear, articulate and well toned, with sufficient compass, pleasingly harmonious', but 'his language is indeed much injured by a strong Scots accent'. Cunningham had no descendants of his own, and his connection to the Westenra family needs unravelling.

General Cunningham served in the army in Ireland. As a very young man he had fought in the Battle of Culloden in 1746. He came to Ireland in the 1750s and for a while was aide-de-camp to the Archbishop of Armagh, a most genial and sociable man named Stone. Stone was a good friend of a certain Lady Blayney. Through his connection to the Archbishop, Cunningham met and married Lady Blayney's daughter Elizabeth Murray, and as a result of his mother-in-law's influence he became a member of parliament at both Dublin and Westminster, representing the constituencies of Tulsk in Roscommonn, Armagh, Monaghan and finally East Grinstead in England.

Lady Blayney was married twice: first to the seventh Lord Blayney, and, after he died, to a wealthy landowner from Monaghan, a Colonel John Murray. Elizabeth was his daughter. Lady Blayney kept on calling herself Lady Blayney until her death. She herself was the daughter of another wealthy landowner in Co. Monaghan: Sir Alexander Cairnes, first baronet. His family also came from Scotland, probably at the time of the Plantation of Ulster by James I at the start of the seventeenth century.

Mary Cairnes was the only child of Sir Alexander Cairnes. She was married at a tender age to the seventh Baron Cadwallader Blayney, a much older man. She had a brother who died young. In 1680 her father had bought the land that was to become the future Rossmore estate outside Monaghan town, from the fifth Lord Blayney, grandfather of Mary's husband-to-be. It was obvious that by marrying the daughter of Sir Alexander, the seventh Lord Blayney would also be regaining the land that had been his family's. It was an extremely unhappy marriage. Writing later to a cousin, a Mrs Lavington, whom she had known as a child, Mary Cairnes says:

> You know my father lost a very considerable fortune in the South Sea [Bubble, in 1720] and at seventeen I left the pleasures of London to live upon a small estate here in Ireland. Two years after, I was married to my Lord Blayney, against my own opinion, he had an agreeable outside, but there was a terrible inside. I endured all sorts of indignity for several years, even frequent blows; after bearing this usage longer than perhaps many others would ... at last I went back to my

father at Monaghan, and never saw my angry dear afterwards. However, two evils that I escaped, supported my spirits very much; I never had a child by a man who I could not
love, and the other was that … my health was preserved.

Three years later her father died, and shortly after that
Cadwallader Blayney also died, leaving her a young childless
widow of twenty-seven. Her father's brother, who became the
second baronet, Sir Harry Cairnes, gave her an adequate income to
live on. She was also his heir, as he had no children.

Very soon after the death of her husband, she married the love
of her life, a relation of hers, Colonel Murray. She says: 'He was the
choice of my reason as well as my heart, and my expectations were
fully satisfied.' After such bad beginnings, Mary's life became ever
more interesting and delightful. Her uncle Harry died, and left her
his considerable fortune and large estates in Co. Monaghan. She
had also inherited a portion of her first husband's estate. She then
proceeded to have five children, all of them daughters, of whom
four survived. Mary's daughters were the foundation stone on
which Mary Westenra's ancestry was built.

Mary, the Dowager Lady Blayney, was by now a woman of considerable influence. It was most important to her that her daughters should marry well, and in the eyes of the world, three out of
the four of them did. (Her fifth daughter died young.) The eldest
daughter, Frances, married William Henry Fortescue, of Co. Louth,
in 1752. He was created the first Lord Clermont in 1770, and seven
years later became the Earl of Clermont. Frances was a considerable heiress, and there is no doubt that her future expectations
helped to further her husband's career. Lady Clermont and her
husband became known for their 'ton' (fashionableness) in London
society. Lord Clermont became a crony of the Prince of Wales (later
George IV). Lady Clermont spent time in Paris and became the
intimate friend of Queen Marie Antoinette. She had no children.
An example of her way of life in London is given in Mrs Delany's
mischievous account: 'My fine neighbour Lady Clermont sent
cards to a few of her acquaintance (not exceeding three hundred)
to drink tea and walk in the park.' Lord Clermont was, according

to Dr Antony Malcomson of the Northern Ireland Public Record Office, 'undoubtedly among the richest men in Ireland'.

Lady Clermont died in 1820. She had inherited the entirety of her mother's fortune when Mary died in 1790, aged eighty-five. Provision had to be made from this estate for her three younger sisters, Elizabeth, Anne and Harriet. Under the terms of Mary's settlement in 1743, her estate went first to her eldest daughter Frances, for as long as she lived, then to her next sister Elizabeth, then to Anne, then to Harriet. If any of them had sons, the sons would inherit in the same order as their mothers, but only after the mothers were dead.

Elizabeth, as we have seen, married the Scottish soldier Robert Cunningham, later the first Lord Rossmore. They had no children. Anne married a wealthy man – Theophilus Jones. Malcomson wrote of them that they were 'sufficiently wealthy in their own right to move in the highest Dublin society'. Harriet's was the least successful marriage. She married a man of Dutch descent – Henry Westenra.

Both Anne Jones and Harriet Westenra produced sons, but Anne's son died tragically when he was a young man, which left Harriet's elder son, Warner William Westenra, as the ultimate heir to Mary Blayney's large estate and fortune. Warner William Westenra became, eventually, the second Baron Rossmore, through the complex arrangements of his grandmother and aunts – which need to be carefully explained.

Elizabeth's husband Robert Cunningham was able to combine his parliamentary life and his soldiering. He was made a general in 1772, a major general in 1777, and colonel of the 5th Royal Irish Dragoons in 1787. In 1793 he was made commander in chief of the army in Ireland. As a result of all this public service, he was granted the title of Baron Rossmore of Monaghan in 1796. It was undoubtedly through the influence of his in-laws, Lady Blayney and the Clermonts, that he was enabled to get the Act of Parliament through that allowed his wife's nephew to inherit the title. He built for himself and his wife a fine new house in Co. Wicklow, known as Mount Kennedy. It still exists, in good order, today. It was finished in 1784. He died suddenly in 1801, after having attended a

Drawing Room – a formal evening of entertainment by the Lord Lieutenant – at Dublin Castle. Sir Jonah Barrington recalled in his memoirs that on the day before he died, Cunningham, seemingly in robust health, invited Lady Barrington and himself to visit Mount Kennedy the next day. That night, the Barringtons retired at about midnight.

> ... towards two in the morning I was awakened by a sound of a very extraordinary nature. I listened; it occurred first at short intervals; it resembled neither a voice nor an instrument, it was softer than any voice, and wilder than any music, and seemed to float in the air. I don't know wherefore, but my heart beat forcibly; the sound became still more plaintive, till it almost died away in the air, when a sudden change, as if excited by a pang, changed its tone; it seemed *descending*. I felt every nerve tremble; it was not a *natural* sound, nor could I make out the point from whence it came.
>
> At length I awakened Lady Barrington, who heard it as well as myself; she suggested that it might be an Eolian harp; but to that instrument it bore no similitude – it was altogether a different *character of sound*. My wife at first appeared less affected than I, but subsequently she was more so.
>
> We now went to a large window in our bedroom which looked directly upon a small garden underneath; the sound seemed then obviously to ascend from a grass-plot immediately below our window. ... At last a deep, heavy, throbbing sigh seemed to issue from the spot, and was shortly succeeded by a sharp but low cry, and by the distinct exclamation, thrice repeated, of 'Rossmore—Rossmore—Rossmore!'

At seven the next morning Sir Jonah and Lady Barrington were awakened with the news that Lord Rossmore had died in the night, suffering his final agonies '*at the moment I heard his name pronounced*'.

After Lord Rossmore's death, his mother-in-law, the redoubtable Mary, Dowager Lady Blayney, came to live near the Cunninghams in Wicklow for the last years of her life. She lived in

Corke Abbey, near Bray, and her youngest daughter Harriet Westenra often came to stay with her. Harriet kept a diary, and from it we learn something of her mother's way of life, and the social events they both attended. She describes dinner parties at Corke Lodge, which often included the Lord Lieutenant of Ireland, who was at that time the Duke of Rutland. She and her daughters were on very close and friendly terms with the owners of great houses in Ireland, often staying with or visiting the Meaths, Waterfords, Clanwilliams, Powerscourts, Leitrims, Leinsters, Langrishes, etc. Harriet tells poignantly of her feeling when her mother died at Corke Abbey on 24 July 1790: 'There went the most extraordinary great and good woman that ever lived, and who, during a life of 85 years, fulfilled every station and relation of it, in a most exemplary manner. I have been a wretch ever since. God grant I may bear this affliction as I ought.'

Lady Blayney was a strong protector of women's rights. Her will had a strange clause in it. Her bequest to her daughters was curious, in so much that no grandson's son was to take an inheritance while any granddaughter remained to take any share, and no daughter could alter this in favour of her son. Another clause showed her lack of religious bigotry. Her books were to be sold to the family if they so desired, and the proceeds were to go to 'her poor tenants in Monaghan *without exception as to religion*'.

Mary's third daughter, Anne, married to the wealthy and influential Theophilus Jones, also lived near her mother in Wicklow, and saw her very often. Had her son not been so tragically killed while travelling abroad as a young man, the future Rossmores would have had the surname Jones instead of Westenra. Theophilus Jones was the grandson of Sir Theophilus Jones, who fought for Charles I in the Irish wars of 1641–53. When Charles II regained the throne in 1660 he ordered that those officers known as 'the forty-nine' who had fought for him and his father, should be paid arrears. Sir Theophilus Jones was one of thirty-three people who were, according to the Act of Settlement of 1660, given a large grant of land, and an annual income of £200 for the rest of his life. This must have been the time when the Joneses started to amass their considerable wealth. Theophilus, the grandson who married

Anne Murray, had land in Meath. He, together with his two broth-ers-in-law, Cunningham and Westenra, represented Monaghan in Parliament: they took it in turns, thanks to the great influence of their mother-in-law Lady Blayney.

Finally, and most vitally for this story, we come to the youngest of the four surviving Murray sisters. Harriet Murray was born in 1742. In 1764 she married Henry Westenra. In direct opposition to the Joneses, Warner and Peter Westenra were listed at the time of Charles I's execution as Soldiers and Adventurers of the Commonwealth. They are listed at this time as 'Westonray (or Westonra)'. Warner, who was the father of Peter, is listed as of King's County and Antrim, and Peter is listed as of Louth and Cork. They are again listed, this time with their name definitely Westenra, in a list of Names of Persons in the Grants, under the Acts of Settlement and Explanation, which were passed between 1661 and 1665. The Acts were passed just after Charles II was restored to the throne, but were supplemental to acts passed by Charles I in 1640 for, among other things, 'the speedy and effec-tual Reducing of Rebels in His Majesty's Kingdom of Ireland'. In this way the dissidents were effectually bought in, by more grants of land. So, by 1662, when they became naturalized citizens of England and Ireland, the Westenra family had the rank and posi-tion of landed gentry in Ireland, and a certain amount of wealth, although when Harriet married Henry Westenra in 1764 he was certainly the least wealthy of the brothers-in-law. Later, when they were living near Dublin, they were very badly off. Malcomson quotes a letter from Lady Clermont describing Westenra in the 1770s as 'almost starving, his wife having hardly a decent gown, and both of them as obliged to avoid the expense of attending social occasions so that they might save sufficient money to send their eldest son to school'.

One of the reasons for this poverty was that Henry's widowed mother, Lady Hester Westenra, the daughter of the Earl of Cavan, was able to engross most of the proceeds from the family estates in King's County and Queen's County. The estate was, in fact, at the time of Henry's death worth £5000 a year, which would eventually come to Henry's sons. It was fortunate that Henry had influential in-laws. Not only Lady Blayney, but his brother-in-law the Earl of Clermont were very good to his wife's relations.

It was very important that Harriet and Henry Westenra's eldest son should be well educated, for he was to become, as the result of his cousin Henry Jones's untimely death, the heir apparent to the Monaghan estates of Lady Blayney, and to the Rossmore title. His name was Warner William Westenra, and he was born in 1765. His uncle by marriage, the first Lord Rossmore, died in 1801, and so Warner William became the second Lord Rossmore when he was thirty-six. Alas, the title brought no wealth with it. General Cunningham (Lord Rossmore) left his house and money to his Cunningham relations – some of whom continued to live at Mount Kennedy until only a few years ago. Poor Warner William had to wait a very long time for his inheritance, for under the terms of his grandmother's will, his aunts had each in succession to inherit the estate, and had to die before he was allowed to inherit anything. Unfortunately for him, they all lived to a ripe old age. Frances Clermont died aged eighty-six in 1820, Elizabeth Rossmore died aged ninety-two in 1827 and Anne Jones also died in 1827, aged eighty-seven. His own mother died in 1822, aged eighty.

Warner William had the frustration of watching 'Queen Bess' and 'Queen Anne', as he called his ancient aunts, maunder on from year to year, while he badly needed his inheritance. In 1823, he was thinking of standing for Parliament for Monaghan. His son Henry wrote to him from England: 'If you court a contest (at the next county election) I know not where the money is to come from. I have it not, I know, nor do I know when I shall have it.'

It was not, in fact, until he was sixty-two, in 1827, that the last aunts died, and he could finally come into his estate, and spend some money on the Rossmore property, which had been the Blayney/Cairnes property, in Monaghan.

In 1827 there was no good house in Rossmore Park. General Cunningham had stayed there sometimes, when he was representing Monaghan in Parliament, but according to Warner William's son Henry, writing to his father in 1823, there was 'only a paltry cabin, unfurnished and mean' as a dwelling place. Warner William, with his inheritance at last, decided to change all that. He employed the well-known architect William Vitruvius Morrison to build him a Tudor-Gothic castle, dominated by a square tower and turret, with crow-step battlements. He lived in this fine creation until his death in 1842, at the age of seventy-seven. He had married twice. His first wife, whom he married in 1791, was Marianne, or Mary Anne, the daughter of Charles Walsh of Walsh Park, Co. Tipperary, a Roman Catholic. His first son, Henry Robert, was born at Walsh Park. Marianne died in 1807, and he married Lady Augusta Charteris, who was the daughter of Lord Elcho, and the sister of the Earl of Wemyss, in 1819. He had no children by his second wife. It was during their marriage that he built his splendid castle, and she died two years before him, in 1840. In 1838 he had been granted an English peerage, following Victoria's coronation. This meant he was the second Lord Rossmore in Ireland, and the first Lord Rossmore in England, and could take his seat at Westminster in the House of Lords. This happened four years before his death.

Warner William Westenra was a most able politician, and of all Mary's ancestors was the one in whom she could take most pride. He was a friend of Daniel O'Connell, the great Irish reformer, who did so much to achieve Catholic Emancipation. William Warner was able to persuade O'Connell's Catholic Association to sponsor his son Henry in the 1826 election, and Henry won one of the two Monaghan seats as a result. At that stage some Roman Catholics were allowed to vote: the 'forty-shilling voters'. Henry's main opponent was his neighbour Charles Leslie of Glaslough, who was strongly anti-Catholic.

On the morning of the election 'Mr. Henry Westenra made his entry into the town accompanied by five or six hundred men equipped with newly-cut sticks and wearing a green sprig in their hats. In front of the procession a mounted man bore the tree of liberty followed by one hundred mounted men. At the end of the marching file of men, a small band of musicians preceded the candidate, Mr. Westenra, who was borne in his carriage by enthusiastic supporters. The party proceeded twice around the Diamond, and passing Mr. Leslie's committee room, they waved threateningly at the occupants ...' There was rioting, which continued all day, until eventually the police fired shots. Three men were killed and a number injured, including some of the police.

Warner William's son Henry Robert, third and second Lord Rossmore (herein I will refer only to Irish titles), was born in 1792, so he inherited his father's title when he was fifty. He, like his father, had had to endure years of waiting for their inheritance – he was thirty-five when his great aunts eventually died – and he had shared his father's anxieties as to lack of funds. But he had married, at the age of eighteen, a remarkable woman. She was Anne Douglas-Hamilton, the illegitimate daughter of the Duke of Hamilton, by his mistress the 'notorious' (according to Burke's Peerage and Baronetage) actress Harriet Pye Bennett. The Duke was devoted to her, and as a result insisted that their daughter should be treated as legitimate. She was always known as 'Lady Anne Douglas-Hamilton', and the Duke's sister, Lady Anne Hamilton, introduced her into society. The Duke left her a considerable fortune, and a very large estate, consisting of part of the Isle of Arran. Her estates in 1885 measured 157,386 acres of the United Kingdom and their rateable value was £73,636 per annum, plus a mineral rate of £67,006. So Henry Robert's finances were helped considerably by his marriage. However, although they were married for twenty-four years, there were no children. Anne died in 1844, and two years later Henry Robert married his first cousin once removed, Josephine, who was also known as Julia. Josephine was the daughter of Henry and Harriet Amelia Lloyd, of Farrinroe. Harriet Amelia's mother was Frances Maria (or Mary Frances), daughter of Henry Rossmore, and sister of Warner William. Mary Frances married Sir John Craven Carden, First Baronet, of Templemore.

Josephine was our Mary's grandmother, and another of her redoubtable female ancestors. Through her Mary got a double dose of Westenra blood. She was very young when she married Henry Robert, who was old enough to be her father. But they swiftly produced a large family, of four sons and two daughters. While this was going on, Henry Robert was, like his father, intent upon having tangible, visible proof of his position and standing in the world. In 1858, when he was sixty-six, he set about making Rossmore Castle even more splendid than his father had left it. It was the fashion then, among the wealthy Anglo-Irish landowners, to build themselves romantic fantasy castles. The leading Irish architect of the day was W.H. Lynn. He was, with another Irish architect, Lanyon, responsible for such splendours as Belfast Castle, built for the Marquis of Donegall; Clandeboye, built for the Marquis of Dufferin and Ava; and Castle Leslie, for the Rossmores' near neighbours the Leslies. Henry Robert employed him to turn his father's Tudor-Gothic castle into a Scottish Renaissance creation of immense size and grandeur. Lynn added a massive tower with a polygonal turret and cupola, a balustraded parapet, and a slender square tower with a spire. The result was an extremely romantic building which boasted at least 117 windows of 53 different shapes and sizes, and a most dramatic silhouette – especially as the castle was set on a hill. A present-day architect, Jeremy Williams, remarked of Rossmore: 'It started as Walter Scott and ended as Disney.'

Henry Robert was sadly not to enjoy this new creation of his for very long, because he died in 1860, only two years after his improvements were completed, at the age of sixty-eight. He was probably the most powerful and distinguished of Mary's male ancestors. Like his father and his grandfather before him he represented Monaghan in parliament, before he became a peer. He became Lord Lieutenant of Co. Monaghan in 1843, as his father had been before him, and as his son Derry was to be after him. In order to enlarge his estates in Ireland, he sold the Hamilton property inherited from his first wife back to the Hamilton family. His son Derry, in his book, regrets this, saying 'it was an ill day when he parted with Arran, for the acquired estates were a poor exchange'.

This is the point at which the Rossmore fortunes gradually began their slow decline. The castle and the estates and much of the wealth were still there, but Henry Robert left behind him a young widow with four young sons, who were only nine, seven, six and five years old, and two little daughters. His widow married again three years later: a Lieutenant Colonel George Stacpoole, whose family lived in Eden Vale, Co. Clare. After they were married they lived in France for a time, in Pau in the Pyrenees, and later moved to Boulogne, but they went back to Monaghan as often as they could, and Derry in his book tells of the daredevil exploits the little boys got up to in the grounds of the castle.

Henry Robert's eldest son, Henry Cairnes, known by the nickname 'Rosie', became the fourth Lord Rossmore at the age of nine. Mary's father was the second son, Derrick Warner William.

Acknowledgments

My first thanks go to Jim Bailey and his wife Barbara, who asked me to research and then write the life of Jim's mother. Jim was most generous with his time and his reminiscences, and in allowing me to raid Mary's precious photograph albums and quote from his forthcoming biography of his father.

Two of Mary's grandsons, David Synnott (son of Anne Bailey) and Count Raben (son of Noreen Bailey) were of enormous help, with facts, photographs and careful scrutiny and criticism of my text. It was Paul Raben who allowed me to use Mary's account of her flight from South Africa to England, and to study her logbooks, as well as ransacking for me his store of family photographs and letters. He was immeasurably helpful.

Mary's nephew Lord Rossmore, and her great-nephew Richard Miles (descended from her younger brother Dick), gave me most valuable help and advice.

Karen Martin and Marilyn Farquharson generously allowed me to use the considerable body of research they had compiled for Jim Bailey before I became part of the project. Bert Aggas was another of Jim's researchers whose work I was glad to be able to use.

Antony Malcomson of the Ulster Record Office gave me help above and beyond the call of duty in researching Mary's ancestry.

Mrs Joyce Sampson most kindly discovered for me the history of Abe Bailey's school, Clewer House, in Windsor, Berkshire.

Others who kindly shared their reminiscences of Mary were her niece Brigid Westenra; her granddaughter Starr Harper; Sir Dennis

Acknowledgments

Hennessy (former chairman of the Bailey Trust in South Africa); and her neighbours in Monaghan, Sir John and Desmond Leslie.

Mike Shaw gave me practical help and encouragement.

My husband, Paddy Falloon, gave me loving help with forebearance throughout the four years of the book's gestation.

Lady Bailey's flight routes,
England to South Africa and back,
March 1928 to January 1929

Statute Miles

0   200   400   600   800   1000

Select Bibliography

Bailey, Jim. *The Life of Abe Bailey*. (Forthcoming.)

Barrington, Jonah. *Recollections of Jonah Barrington*. Dublin: Talbot Press, n.d.

Bence-Jones, Mark. *Life in an Irish Country House*. London: Constable, 1996.

———. *Twilight of the Ascendancy*. London: Constable, 1987.

Bennett, Benjamin. *Down Africa's Skyways*. London: Hutchinson, 1932.

Boase, Wendy. *The Sky's the Limit: Women Pioneers in Aviation*. London: Osprey, 1979.

Cadogan, Mary. *Women with Wings*. London: Macmillan, 1992.

de Havilland, Geoffrey. *Sky Fever*. London: Hamish Hamilton, 1961.

Escott, Beryl. *Women in Air Force Blue*. Yeovil: Patrick Stephens, 1989.

Fingall, Elizabeth, Countess of. *Seventy Years Young*. Dublin: Lilliput Press, 1991.

Foster, R.F. *Modern Ireland 1600–1972*. London: Allen Lane, 1988.

Leslie, Anita. *Edwardians in Love*. London: Hutchinson, 1972.

Leslie, Sir Shane. *The Film of Memory*. London: Michael Joseph, 1938

Livingstone, Peadar. *The Monaghan Story*. Enniskillen: Clogher Historical Society, 1980.

Lockhart, J.G., and C.M. Woodhouse. *Rhodes*. London: Hodder and Stoughton, 1963.

Lomax, Judy. *Women of the Air*. London: John Murray, 1986.

Longford, William H. *Who's Who in Aviation History*. Shrewsbury: Airlife, 1994.

Malcomson, A.P.W. *The Clogher Road: The Earl of Clermont, a Forgotten Co. Monaghan Magnate of the Late Eighteenth Century*. Belfast: Ulster Records Office, 1973.

Moorhouse, Edward. *The History and Romance of the Derby*. London: The Biographical Press, 1911.

O'Hart, John. *Irish Landed Gentry*. Shannon: Irish University Press, 1969.

O'Faolain, Sean. *The Irish*. Harmondsworth: Pelican, 1969.

Select Bibliography

Penrose, Harold. *British Aviation: Widening Horizons, 1930–1934*. London: Her Majesty's Stationery Office, 1979.

Richardson, Ethel M. *Long Forgotten Days Leading to Waterloo*. London, 1928.

Rossmore, Lord. *Things I Can Tell*. London: Eveleigh Nash, 1912.

Russell, Mary. *The Blessings of a Good Thick Skirt: Women Travellers and Their World*. London: Collins, 1986.

Smith, Alan, ed. *My Dear Old Abe: Letters to Sir Abe Bailey, 1940*. Lanseria: Clewer Press, 1987.

Smith, Victor. *Open Cockpit Over Africa*. Cape Town: Fair Cape Books, 1992.

Somerville-Large, Peter. *The Irish Country House: A Social History*. London: Sinclair-Stevenson, 1995.

Taylor, J. Wallace. *The Rossmore Incident*. Dublin: Hodges Figgis, 1884.

Thomas, Antony. *Rhodes: The Race for Africa*. New York: St Martin's Press, 1996.

Williams, Jeremy. *Architecture in Ireland 1837–1921*. Dublin: Irish Academic Press, 1994.

Wheatcroft, Geoffrey. *The Randlords*. London: Weidenfeld and Nicolson, 1985.

Index

Mary's many paternal ancestors mentioned in the Appendix but not in the main text are not indexed here